The
GOLDEN RETRIEVER

EDITED BY
MARUICE SHORTMAN

BEST of
BREED

ACKNOWLEDGEMENTS
The publishers would like to acknowledge the following for help with photography: Dogs for the Disabled, Guide Dogs for the Blind Association, Hearing Dogs for Deaf People, Pets As Therapy, Lynn Kipps, Kim Ellis (Tenfield), Sara Woodward (Wyle Valley), Maurice and Judy Shortman (Bridgefarm), Bernard Pound, Angie Cooper (Dikeadaze), and David Tomlinson.

Cover photo: © Tracy Morgan Animal Photography (www.animalphotographer.co.uk)
page 62 © istockphoto.com/Mark Coffey

The British Breed Standard reproduced in Chapter 7 is the copyright of the Kennel Club and published with the club's kind permission. Extracts from the American Breed Standard are reproduced by kind permission of the American Kennel Club.

THE QUESTION OF GENDER
**The 'he' pronoun is used throughout this book instead of the rather impersonal 'it',
but no gender bias is intended.**

First published in 2008 by The Pet Book Publishing Company Limited
The Granary, Bishton Farm, Tidenham, Chepstow, Gloucestershire NP16 7LJ
Reprinted in 2010.

This edition published in 2012 by The Pet Book Publishing Company Limited.

ISBN
978-1-906305-40-6
1-906305-40-4

Printed and bound in China through Printworks Int. Ltd.

CONTENTS

GETTING TO KNOW GOLDEN RETRIEVERS

The Golden Retriever is an intelligent, loyal companion, who wants nothing more than to be part of the family. Originally bred as a working gundog, the Golden's job was to search for, find and retrieve game. He is, therefore, an active, athletic dog, with the stamina to work all day, often in harsh conditions. But more importantly, the Golden needed to work closely with his handler, and so he was bred to be biddable, trustworthy and confident. These characteristics are the hallmarks of the Golden Retriever's outstanding temperament, and they are what have made him an ideal companion dog.

PHYSICAL CHARACTERISTICS

The Golden Retriever is a breed without exaggeration; he is balanced and symmetrical, and

What makes a Golden Retriever so special?

appears sound and well put together. When moving, he should look powerful, with long, free strides. Golden Retriever males are bigger than the females; a dog should be between 56-61 cm (22-24 inches) at the withers (the top of the shoulders) and a bitch is 51-56 cm (20-22 inches).

One of the most beautiful aspects of the breed is its colour. The Golden Retriever comes in a full range of colours from pale cream through every shade of gold to dark gold. The coat can be flat or wavy, with full feathering on the neck, chest, tummy, legs and tail. The coat has two layers: a long top coat, and a dense, water-resistant undercoat that protected him from the cold, particularly when he was retrieving from water.

The typical weight for a male Golden in good physical condition is approximately 29.5 to 32 kg (65-70 lb) and a female is between 25 to 27 kg (55-60 lb). An overweight animal is far unhealthier than an animal that is slightly underweight; a good guide is that the ribs should be well covered, but you should be able to feel the last rib. At 12 to 24 months, a growing Golden will go through a teenage stage, and will appear underweight and gawky. Goldens tend to mature in mind and body later than spaniels and Labrador Retrievers.

TYPICAL BEHAVIOUR

All dogs are individuals, and there are lots of different Golden Retriever personalities. However, there seems to be a number of Golden Retriever behaviours that are special to the breed.

Goldens are famous for their love of presenting 'gifts' to visitors. This is a very common

The Golden Retriever is an active, powerful dog that is balanced and symmetrical in build.

trait in the breed, and owners returning home will also be greeted with a present. A Golden is not fussy about the nature of the gift – it's whatever comes to hand at the time, be it a cushion, a toy, or stolen socks from the wash basket. It may not always be a gift you want, but few can resist the wagging tail and delight of a Golden who is bearing a gift.

Goldens are also good gardeners; if allowed, they will watch patiently while you plant out your bedding plants – and when you have finished they will dig them all back out for you!

Goldens also enjoy trench work, and will dig deep into your lawn, given the opportunity. If you want to preserve your garden, it is best to have a Golden-free zone that will be safe from your dog's attentions.

The best thing for a Golden Retriever is to be included in family activities, and a trip in the car is considered a highlight of the day. A Golden doesn't mind if you are not going anywhere interesting – he just likes the trip out and the feeling of being included. If you leave your car parked in the drive, with the hatchback open, you can be sure

that your Golden will jump in and sit contentedly in the car, regardless of the fact that it is going nowhere!

The Golden Retriever was bred to retrieve from water, and most Goldens have a love of water and will take the plunge at any given opportunity; they are not always too fussy about the cleanliness of their chosen bath. If you want to keep your Golden Retriever clean and dry you will need to spot water before he does! I have known a Golden Retriever to wallow in a single mud puddle in an otherwise arid stretch of land.

Goldens are great swimmers – and if there is water, a Golden Retriever will find it...

A typical Golden greeting, bearing a special 'gift'.

The kindly Golden lives in harmony with other pets.

THE GOLDEN MIND

Golden Retrievers are sociable, intelligent animals; they prefer company, human or otherwise. If a Golden's intelligence is neglected and he is left home alone, he will use his brains to his own ends. This can make result in an unruly, destructive and noisy creature. However, with training, socialisation, and company, a Golden is a joy to live with. A little time and effort is needed at the beginning to rear a dog you can enjoy and take anywhere. All dogs need discipline and structure to their lives; they are pack animals and need the security of pack behaviour. You need to be pack leader and all the humans in

the family must be above the dog in the pack order, including children.

Children need to be taught respect for the animal and the animal's feelings. A child must learn that the dog is not a toy and can be hurt by rough treatment, such as pulling and prodding. Equally, the dog needs to respect the child as a superior in the pack order. This can be reinforced by such measures as ensuring a dog and child do not share food, and that the dog obeys house rules, such as not jumping on the sofa when children are around. If a good relationship is established at an early stage, a Golden Retriever

will have a very special place in the family circle.

The Golden Retriever is kindly and tolerant and will get on with other pets in the family. My dogs have lived in harmony with family cats and pet ducks, but I have found that next door's cat is still fair game for chasing out of their garden! But as long as a Golden is fully socialised with the outside world, he will greet other dogs, other animals, and other people as he would family members.

Generally, the Golden Retriever is an easy dog to train; he is eager to please and will enjoy spending quality time with you in training sessions. However, the

Golden can sometimes by a little stubborn – this may well be a sign of a bright dog taking advantage of his owner. If your Golden decides to dig his heels in, do not become confrontational. The best plan is to ask him to do something different; this will have the effect of shifting his mind-set, and you will be able to reward him for doing as you ask. (For more information on training and socialisation, see Chapter Six.)

MORE THAN ONE?

Golden Retrievers seem to be collectable; people start off with one – but not for long! If you decide you want more than one Golden, resist the temptation of buying two together. Allow for a minimum 12-month gap between puppies, as you need time to train and bond with one puppy at a time or they will rely on each other. They will be like twins and will have a unique connection with each other rather than

bonding with you. In the same way as it is much easier to have three children with two-year plus gaps in between, so it is much better to train one dog to your liking before beginning with another. The second dog will be easier to train, and will, hopefully, learn a lot from the older, well-behaved adult animal.

AN IDEAL HOME

A Golden Retriever will adapt to town living or country living, as

Goldens are very collectable – and they will live happily as a group.

long as he has regular exercise. Remember that the Golden is a coated breed and will shed blond hairs on carpets and on your clothing. When a Golden is out exercising, his coat will absorb water and dirt, which will then be brought into the house. If you are house-proud, you will need to rinse your dog's coat when he returns from exercise, and then brush out the dirt when it is dry.

Once fully grown, a Golden is easy to exercise even if you do have access to country walks. As a retrieving breed, the Golden will love a game of ball or Frisbee in the local park, and this is fun for both dog and owner.

WORKING GUNDOGS

Originally developed to be a shooting companion, the Golden Retriever was primarily used for retrieving game. Today, Goldens are out-numbered in the shooting world by Labrador Retrievers and English Springer Spaniels, but the working Golden Retriever is still very popular, and it is a pleasure to see him doing the job for which he was intended.

Golden Retrievers air-scent, whereas spaniels hunt with their noses very close to the ground, looking very busy and workmanlike. Labrador Retrievers hunt with their noses slightly higher from the ground, and

Goldens higher again, which I find very helpful in poor scenting conditions, and when working in cover such as sugar beet, kale, stubble, or turnips.

The Golden Retriever can be used for three different jobs in the shooting field:

- Beaters' dogs, helping to flush the game forward to the guns.
- Picking-up dogs, working with their handlers to collect dead and wounded game from behind the guns.
- Peg dogs, where the dog sits by his handler's side while he is shooting, and then at the end of the drive he is sent out to retrieve shot game.

The Golden Retriever works with great enthusiasm when called on to hunt and retrieve.

The show-bred Golden Retriever is heavier in build and has more coat than a Golden from working lines.

Photo: Lynn Kipps.

The working-bred Golden Retriever is built for speed.

The picking-up dogs hunt out the fallen game in woodland, water and undergrowth. The Golden Retriever uses his amazing scenting ability to locate the shot game, which would be very hard to find. A Golden will search and then retrieve the game to his handler. Wounded game will sometimes run off into the undergrowth, and the dog soon learns to follow the scent, and catch and retrieve the bird, so that it can be quickly and humanely despatched. Without the gundogs, these birds would not be found and many would be left to suffer.

THE GREAT DIVIDE
When the breed was developing, Golden Retrievers were often dual purpose, and a dog could make his mark in the show ring and also compete in field trials at the highest level. These days the breed has split into two types. Working dogs are bred to compete in field trials, and working tests, and are used for rough shooting, and show dogs are bred specifically for the show ring. It is the show-bred Goldens that are generally sold for pets. The working-bred dogs tend to be finer in build, longer on the leg, and not so heavily coated as

Golden Retrievers from show lines. The show-bred dogs are heavier set, squarer animals, whereas working dogs are very athletic and are built for speed. Both show and working Goldens share the same confident, friendly temperament, but dogs from working lines do need more mental stimulation. If a dog from working lines is not being used in the field, he should have some other outlet for his energies, such as being trained in competitive obedience or agility.

Despite the acknowledged division between Golden

BRIDGING THE DIVIDE

I have been working my show-bred Golden Retrievers to the gun and in working tests since 1990. It all started when the Midland Golden Retriever Club organised gundog training classes in a Birmingham park one evening a week, and I went along. I did not have a clue what to expect, and did not appreciate the Golden's connection to gundog work. I knew that Golden Retrievers belonged to the Gundog Group in the show world, but I never really thought about the implications of this.

We started out with basic obedience, then moved on to retrieving canvas dummies, and introduction to the noise of a starting pistol to simulate gunshot on a game shoot. (This would no longer be allowed in a public area, as you would be arrested for having a replica firearm.) The training classes were a great starting point, and I came to realise that basic obedience and sensible introduction to gunshot are the two most important aspects of gundog training.

There is a lot more to gundog work than 'retrieving'. The retrieve should be the reward for complying with the commands, and it should not be all about thrown objects. I would expect my dogs to retrieve chosen objects placed on the floor while the dog is left in a sit-stay, then, on returning, the dog would be sent for the object or walked at heel away from the object, then sent to retrieve.

I am lucky enough to live in the middle of a game shoot, and after a summer of gundog training I approached our local gamekeeper and asked if I could go on a shoot. He took me on to another local shoot so that he could show me what to do, how to behave and how to stay safe.

Training for the dogs continued, as it is a big jump from retrieving a canvas dummy, filled with sawdust, to freshly shot game. I now use cold game (game shot and taken home to be used for training) for youngsters to prepare them for freshly shot birds.

I believe that all Golden Retrievers – show or

Retrievers from working lines and those from show lines, there are many kennels that try to breed a dual-purpose dog, attempting to maintain the intelligence and natural retrieving ability, but also conforming to the Kennel Club Breed Standard (see Chapter 7: The Perfect Golden Retriever). A lot of Golden Retriever breeders and owners do not have the opportunity to work their dogs in the shooting field, although I feel, given the opportunity from a

young age, many show-bred Goldens possess the ability to work, if not all with the speed and style of working-bred dogs.

VERSATILE GOLDENS

The Golden Retriever has a biddable nature that makes him ideal for a number of jobs. As well as the traditional role of shooting companion, the Golden has become the chosen breed in many different and challenging careers. His excellent sense of smell is put

to use in 'sniffer' detector work, and for search and rescue. His kindly, gentle nature is well suited to working as an assistance dog; he is widely used as a guide dog, a dog for the disabled, a therapy dog, and for seizure alert (giving people advance warning of an oncoming fit). A very popular breed in the show ring, often attracting the highest entries, the Golden Retriever is also a champion in the other disciplines, such as field trials, obedience and working bred – have the potential to work in the shooting field, but not all owners have the access and connections to allow this. As for competition work (i.e.; workingtests and field trials – a balanced, agile show-bred dog can hold his own; he just needs more patient sensitive handling. For example, a young Golden Retriever may find it hard to maintain a Sit-Stay because he cannot cope with being left. In this instance, it is better to loop the lead round his neck to stop him running in on a retrieve until sent. This is effective, and as the dog matures he will learn to respond to the command and not need the restraint.

Golden Retrievers mature in their minds slower than spaniels and Labrador Retrievers, and I find show-bred dogs slower still. I judge each dog on his willingness to please, and on the strength of his character. I have found that it is often the slower, quieter dogs that turn out the best because they are doing it to please you, and not for themselves.

These show-bred Golden Retrievers have proved their worth working in the field.

agility (see Chapter Six: Training and Socialisation).

SNIFFER DOGS

Sniffer dogs or detector dogs are used by numerous agencies, including Customs, the armed forces, the police, the fire service, the prison service, and even schools. The Golden Retriever is highly trainable and has proved very effective in this work.

Sniffer dogs are used to detect all manner of items, such as explosives, guns and ammunition, drugs, large amounts of money, ivory, meat and tobacco products. The fire service uses them to detect arson, and the prison service has started using them to detect mobile phones. In the USA, they are being trained to find large quantities of DVDs, to help in the fight against counterfeiting.

The dogs are taught using a simple game of hide-and-seek. Their hunting skills are used to pick up a scent and find hidden items; they are then rewarded with either their favourite toy or titbits and plenty of praise. If the dogs are searching for drugs, they are taught to hunt out anything with that scent, and then to sit and stare at the location until the handler retrieves the item and then rewards the dog.

SEARCH AND RESCUE

With search and rescue, the dogs are taught to 'hunt' for people.

Golden Retrievers excel at this task, with their excellent scenting ability and their eagerness to work for their handlers. Search and rescue is also based on a hide-and-seek game that, once perfected, could be a matter of life or death. Search and rescue dogs are trained to find missing people by following scent that is carried on the air. The dogs are used on all types of terrain to search for mountain climbers, for lost or injured walkers, to help track criminals, or to find a lost child. In many cases, a dog will travel with his handler by helicopter; the dog soon gets used to being winched in and out. It is also common for search and rescue teams to be deployed to countries in the event of a disaster, helping to search for people who have been buried following an earthquake or a terrorist attack.

Between 250 and 350 search dogs were used in the search for survivors in the 9/11 terrorist attack on the Twin Towers and the Pentagon. A Golden Retriever named Riley made the headlines when pictures and video footage of him being winched in and out of the area in a cradle were shown worldwide. Riley is a member of the Pennsylvania fire fighters search team and was winched 60 feet above the Twin Towers site.

The training for search and rescue work starts at an early age. Puppies are selected and socialised with people and other dogs. They are taught basic obedience and 'stock familiarisation'. This means that when hillsides and large areas of countryside are searched, the dogs must show no interest in any types of stock grazing nearby. The second stage of training is to 'find'. Volunteers called

'dogsbodies' are used so the trainee dogs can practise searching for a body. The dog will indicate a 'find' by barking to alert his handler. The third stage of the training is for the handler to be taught how to search areas with their dog. At first the handlers know where the 'dogsbodies' are located, but, as they progress, they will not be told the location.

GUIDE DOGS

The Golden Retriever is highly valued as a guide dog for the blind. There are approximately 5,000 guide dog partnerships in the United Kingdom at any one time, and the Guide Dogs for the Blind Association has its own breeding programme, breeding more than 1,000 puppies each year. Puppies are socialised with families for the first year, and they then go forward to specialised training. The trainee guide dogs must learn:
* To walk in a straight line in the centre of the pavement
* Not to turn corners unless told to do so
* To stop at kerbs and wait for the command to cross the road, or turn left or right
* To judge height and width so that the owner is not in danger
* To ignore a command to go forward if there is danger, such as an oncoming vehicle.

After completing training, the dog is matched with a blind owner. Matching the correct dog with the correct owner takes skill and experience. The owner's length of stride, height and

Golden Retrievers formed part of the search and rescue team that was called in following the terrorist attack on the Twin Towers.
Photo: LA Times.

lifestyle all are taken into consideration when choosing the dog. The pair then spend up to four weeks in intensive training until they qualify as a fully fledged partnership. The working life of a guide dog is around seven years, after which the dog retires to live with his blind owner as a pet. If this is not practical, the retired dog will be placed with voluntary 'adopters'. Dogs that are unsuitable for guide dog work are quite often found alternative work with Hearing Dogs, Dogs for the Disabled or the police.

The breeds most frequently used as guide dogs are Labrador Retrievers and Golden Retrievers, or first crosses between the two, which have proved to be very successful.

HEARING DOGS

Golden Retrievers also work as hearing dogs for this purpose. Training dogs for deaf people started in the United States, and was launched in the UK at Crufts in 1982. Hearing dogs can be any shape and size and are more often than not selected from rescue centres. The Golden Retriever is quick to learn and highly responsive, and makes an excellent choice for this type of work.

A hearing dog needs to be alert and full of enthusiasm, with the will to please. He is taught to get excited and react to sounds, and then to alert his owner. Just as a dog gets excited when you get out his lead, as he associates it with 'walkies', or when you get out his bowl ready for feeding, so these

The Golden Retriever is regularly used as a guide dog for the blind.

dogs' enthusiasm is channelled into sound. They are taught using the clicker training method, originally used to train dolphins and now widely used in dog training. The dogs are trained to react to sounds using food, praise or toys as rewards. On hearing certain sounds (such as an alarm clock, doorbell, telephone, cooker timer, or a baby crying) a hearing dog is taught to seek out his deaf owner and touch them with his paw. The owner then asks, "What is it?", and the dog leads them to the source of the noise.

The dog is also trained to react to danger sounds, such as the smoke alarm, fire alarm, carbon

monoxide alarm, and burglar alarm. In these cases the dog is trained to touch the owner with his paw, and then lie down. This is a special 'alert signal' to indicate danger.

ASSISTANCE DOGS

Golden Retrievers work with people with a range of disabilities; the scheme has proved so successful that it has been extended to include children. Goldens and Labradors are the most commonly used breeds, as well as Golden-Labrador crosses. In the UK, assistance dogs are trained by Canine Partners and by Dogs for the Disabled. The dogs

WORKING GOLDENS

An assistance dog will help his partner in a variety of different situations.

Hearing dog Zak: One of a number of Golden Retrievers currently working with hearing impaired people in the UK.

start their training at around eight weeks old and are donated or bought from a number of breeders that work closely with the charity. As with the other charities, puppies are placed with a volunteer puppy socialiser for the first 12 months and are introduced to life, basic obedience, house training, public transport, people and noises. Then, at around 12 months, they start a six- to eight-month training programme. The first three months is spent with a trainer, learning important task work, which includes:

• Obedience: This is required for all the dog's work, learning to settle in environments such as 'the office' or a restaurant. The dog must also get used to wheelchairs and walking next to crutches.

• Pushing: This is taught using the dog's own natural behaviours. A dog will naturally pounce at things, and this skill is used to push buttons, such as alarm buttons, light switches or the button on pedestrian crossings.

• Pulling: This starts with a game of tug, and, trained through a reward system, can be used to pull open doors (using a specially adapted rope door handle) and remove items of clothing, such as socks, gloves, shoes, coats and even trousers.

• Retrieving: The dog is trained to pick up dropped items, such as keys, a phone, a remote control or a book. He can also be used to bring in the milk, fetch the post or papers, empty the washing machine, or even fetch crutches. And no matter how often the owner asks him to fetch items, the dog just thinks it's an enjoyable game.

• Speak: The last thing the dogs are taught is to speak on command. This can be used to raise the alarm if the owner has fallen. It is also used at shops or offices if access is a problem and the dog needs to attract attention in order to get help.

The last three months of training is spent with the new owner and the trainer, and the dog is matched with the potential new owner according to the person's specific needs. For example, an owner who needed a lot of things to be picked up would be matched with a dog that particularly enjoyed retrieve work.

The gentle nature of a Golden Retriever makes him ideal for therapy work.

Best of all, the Golden Retriever is an outstanding companion dog.

THERAPY DOGS

In the UK, therapy dogs are known as PAT dogs after the organising charity, Pets As Therapy. The Golden Retriever's gentle disposition comes into its own in this type of work, where dogs visit hospital patients and residents of other long-stay institutions. The health and psychological benefits of these visits is now well documented, and it is very rewarding to see the comfort and companionship that therapy dogs bring to people who are unable to keep their own pets.

The only criteria for a therapy dog is that he must have been with his owner for at least six months, and the dog must be over nine months old. Before starting work, a prospective therapy dog must pass a temperament test, which is conducted by one of a nationwide team of assessors.

The owner must be able to demonstrate control over their dog while holding a conversation, as much of the volunteer's time is spent talking with clients.

SEIZURE ALERT DOGS

These dogs are trained to respond and alert their owners to imminent epileptic seizures. A seizure alert dog will give his owner a signal many minutes before the onset of a seizure, thus allowing the person a chance to get to a place of safety. This obviously gives the owner increased security and independence. It is thought that the dogs react to minute body changes in the owner, which are so minute that the owner is not aware of them. Some dogs alert their owners by barking; there is one Golden working as a seizure alert dog who uses his paw and prods his owner to give a warning.

When the dog is being paired with his new owner, the trainer will watch the dog and owner on CCTV, and then tell the owner how the dog is reacting prior to the seizure so that the owner knows what to look for.

Not only do these dogs help their owners in many practical ways, but they also provide social, psychological and physical benefits – and last and not least, companionship and love.

SUMMARY

The Golden Retriever is truly an outstanding breed, combining beauty and brains. But most important of all, he is gentle, loving and full of fun, making him the perfect companion.

THE FIRST GOLDEN RETRIEVERS

Chapter 2

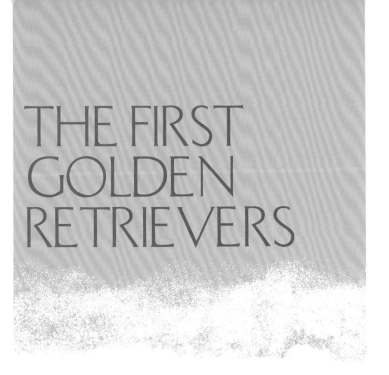

Over the years, many eminent breed archivists have researched the origin and evolution of the Golden Retriever in the United Kingdom and throughout the world. However, much of the credit must be given to the late Mrs Elma Stonex for the vast amount of time and energy she dedicated to defining the origins of the Golden Retriever. Mrs Stonex researched in depth, over a period of 10 years, with the aid of the sixth Earl of Ilchester, and the result of this research will remain the authority on the genealogy of the breed. Mrs Stonex's findings were eventually published in 1959, showing indisputable evidence that confirmed the origin of the Golden Retriever as a true Scottish breed. This evidence was presented to the Kennel Club in 1960 and was duly accepted.

Henry Edward, fifth Earl of Ilchester, pictured with Ada.

NAMING THE BREED

Following the death of the first Lord Tweedmouth in 1894, the Guisachan Estate became the home of the second Lord Tweedmouth until it was subsequently sold in 1908. There were no breeding records kept for the 'Flat or Wavy Coated Retriever' for the 11 years from 1894 until 1905. However, in 1905 the recording of detailed pedigrees commenced. This coincided with the foundation of the famous Culham kennel, owned by Lord Harcourt. According to evidence found by Mrs Stonex, two puppies were purchased from John MacLennan, a keeper at Guisachan. This evidence was verified in a letter written in 1946 by John MacLennan confirming that Lord Harcourt had bought the puppies from him when he was living at Kerrow House. Kerrow House was on the Guisachan Estate, and leased to John MacLennan by Lord Tweedmouth.

In the early 1900s, activity among breed enthusiasts was restricted to a few breeders. These included Mrs W.M. Charlesworth (Noranby) and Lord Harcourt (Culham), who were instrumental in forming the Golden Retriever Club in 1911. The Flat or Wavy Coated Retrievers were subject to a name change and, in 1913, were registered by the Kennel Club as Retrievers (Golden or Yellow). In 1920, the 'yellow' was dropped and they became known as Retrievers (Golden) – the name we use today.

A SCOTTISH BREED

Prior to Mrs Stonex's work in the 1950s, there were a number of theories circulating about the origin of the Golden Retriever, but all without credence. We know that the first Golden Retrievers were born at Guisachan, which is located in Inverness-shire, near Loch Ness in Scotland. In 1854, Sir Dudley Coutts Marjoribanks (pronounced Marshbanks) purchased the 20,000-acre estate for £52,000, as it was ideal for his sporting activities. Sir Dudley received a peerage and became the first Lord Tweedmouth, and ever since that time, his family have been associated with developing the breed we now know as the Golden Retriever. We are fortunate that the first Lord Tweedmouth was an efficient record-taker, and we have documented evidence of the breed's development in his stud books and their accompanying notes.

The story of the Golden Retriever begins with a dog called Nous, who was a yellow Wavy Coated Retriever – the only yellow dog in a litter of black Wavy Coats. He came from Brighton, and was bred by Lord Chichester. Lord Tweedmouth wanted to develop his own line of working gundogs who would be ideally suited to hunting and retrieving game at Guisachan, and when he saw Nous, walking in the streets of Brighton, he was determined to buy him. Lord Tweedmouth took Nous back to Scotland and in 1868 he was mated to Belle, a Tweed Water Spaniel from the Ladykirk area on the River Tweed. The result was a litter of four yellow pups, recorded as Crocus (the only dog), Cowslip, Primrose and Ada. Lord Tweedmouth retained Cowslip and Primrose at

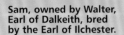

Sam, owned by Walter, Earl of Dalkeith, bred by the Earl of Ilchester.

Culham Copper: Sire of Ch. Noranby Campfire.

Guisachan, while Crocus was given to his son, the Honourable Edward Marjoribanks (later to become the second Lord Tweedmouth), and Ada was given to the fifth Earl of Ilchester and was to become the foundation bitch of the 'Ilchester' line.

Lord Tweedmouth continued to line-breed his stock back to this original litter. However, he did occasionally use an outcross, including mating Cowslip back to a Tweed Water Spaniel named Tweed. Later, in 1875, Cowslip was mated to an Irish Setter belonging to Lord Tweedmouth's son, and Jack and Jill were born.

Lord Tweedmouth bred many litters between 1868 and 1889, with varying results, although the last recorded litter, bred in 1889, produced Prim and Rose. It was written in Lord Tweedmouth's notes that he outcrossed one of his yellow retriever bitches to a Bloodhound in the 1890s. According to Lord Ilchester, this was probably correct but written evidence to support this mating was not available.

EARLY PIONEERS

In 1912, Mrs Charlesworth's bitch Normanby Beauty, of unknown pedigree, was mated to Lord Harcourt's Culham Copper. Culham Copper was bred by Lord Harcourt and sired by Culham Brass out of Culham Rossa. This mating produced the first Champion in the breed, Ch. Noranby Campfire. It should be noted that Mrs Charlesworth's Kennel Club registered affix was originally Normanby but later, for reasons unknown, was changed to Noranby.

Breeders in these formative years often mated very close relatives (in-breeding), such as brother to sister or father to daughter, for two major reasons. Firstly, to establish the breed and form a 'type' and, secondly, due to the very limited bloodlines available, their choice was limited. Other early breeders became established and made their mark either in the field or in the show ring – sometimes both. Amongst these were Mr J. Eccles (Haulstone), Mr W.S. Hunt (Ottershaw), Hon. D. Carnegie (Heydown) and Mr H. Jenner (Abbots). It was Mr Jenner who purchased, from Mr W.S. Hunt, Rory of Bentley, the dog who sired Ch. Michael of Moreton. This great dog went on to win 17 Challenge Certificates.

The First World War prevented the continuation of canine activities between 1914 and 1918. However, there was a small group of dedicated breeders who retained good stock, which helped to establish the breed following the end of the war. Mr Jenner did not breed his dogs after the war, although he did show and judge, and he maintained an interest in the breed until his death.

INFLUENTIAL BLOODLINES IN THE 1920-1930s

The Golden Retrievers of today can all be traced back through their pedigrees to one or more of four very early matings that took place in the early 1920s. These matings were:

Ch. Noranby Diana, born 1929: One of a line of Noranby Champions.

- Glory of Fyning to Stagden Cross Pamela
- Dual Champion Balcombe Boy to Balcombe Bunty
- Binks of Kentford to Balvaig
- Rory of Bentley to Aurora

The impact of these four matings was confirmed in the work that Mrs Stonex did when writing the extended pedigrees in the 1950s. All dedicated Golden Retriever breeders and owners, in the UK and overseas, owe so much to the achievements of Mrs Stonex. Although in a book of this size, it is impossible to mention every important kennel and every influential dog of the formative years, we will mention some of the many kennels that came to the fore in the 1920s.

One of the most influential kennels belonged to Mrs

Cottingham (Woolley) who owned 11 Champions including Ch. Cubbington Diver, winner of 15 Challenge Certificates (CCs) and the sire of five Champions. Mrs Charlesworth and her Noranby kennel continued to win both in the field and in the ring, breeding eight Champions, including the already mentioned Ch. Noranby Campfire. Mrs Charlesworth was involved with the breed for almost 50 years, showing, judging and taking part in field trials until her death. Mr and Mrs Evers-Swindell's Speedwell kennel, which was established in 1921, had a huge influence on the breed in the UK and worldwide. Their foundation sire was Ch. Cornelius. The kennel continued to produce many Champions through the 1920s, including Ch. Speedwell Beryl, Ch. Kelso of Aldgrove, Ch. Speedwell Molly, Ch. Speedwell Brandy, Sh. Ch. Speedwell Emerald, and the first American Champion, Ch. Speedwell Pluto who went on to become a Canadian Champion.

The famous Yelme kennel of Major and Mrs Wentworth-Smith began in 1926 and went on to produce many Champions and field trial winners, including Ch. Bingo of Yelme who became a Champion in America. The first

Golden Retriever to become a Dual Champion, winning honours in the field and in the show ring, was Dual Ch. Balcombe Boy. He was born in 1919, bred by Viscount Harcourt, and he completed both his titles three years later, handled and trained by his owner, Mr R. Herman.

The Rev. E. Needham-Davies (Sundawn) purchased two Goldens from Mr Hunt early in the 1920s, but his most successful dogs were Ch. Sundawn Dancer, purchased from Major Metcalfe, and Sundawn Susie, purchased from Mrs Eccles. Later, Sundawn Dainty – Susie's daughter – was mated to Ch. Sundawn Dancer. This mating produced Gilder, one of the first paler-coated Goldens who was to become a very famous and influential dual-purpose sire.

Mrs I. Parsons started the Torrdale kennel in the 1930s with the purchase of Dukeries Dancing Lady from Mr Jenner. This bitch later became a Champion. Mrs Parsons went on to breed and campaign a number of Champions, including the top-winning bitch of the era, Ch. Torrdale Betty, who won 14 Challenge Certificates.

The Stubbings kennel, owned by Mrs A. Nairn, rose to prominence in the 1930s. She bred many Champions, and a number had a huge influence on the breed, including Stubbings Lorelei, Ch. Stubbings Golden Gloria, Stubbings Golden Gem,

THE GREAT MICHAEL OF MORETON

In the mid 1920s, Mr R. Kirk purchased Michael of Moreton from his breeder, Mr H. Jenner of the Abbots kennel. Mr Kirk was highly rewarded, as Michael went on to become a Champion, winning more Challenge Certificates than any other Golden prior to World War Two. Michael was also successful in field trials; he won the Crufts Gold Trophy and became a highly influential sire.

Ch. Michael of Moreton: Winner of 17 Challenge Certificates.

Ch. Ulvin Vintage of Yelme: The Yelme kennel was successful in the run up to the Second World War, and continued to thrive in the post-war era.

Ch. Deerflite of Yeo: The 'of Yeo' kennel made a significant impact on the breed over six decades.

and Stubbings Golden Kraken. Kraken was the great-grandsire of the first post-war Dual Champion, Stubblesdown Golden Lass, and was also the great-great-grandsire of Ch. Alresford Advertiser. Mrs Elma Stonex purchased her first Golden in 1931 from the Stubbings kennel and the following year bought her foundation bitch, Sally of Perrott. Although winning just one CC, Sally will be remembered as being the dam of Dorcas Bruin sired by Ch. Davie of Yelme.

It was also in the late 1930s that Lucille Sawtell started the 'of Yeo' kennel in the south-west of England. The first Golden in the 'of Yeo' kennel was Princess of Slat, who was bred by Miss Collum. She was by Dual Ch. Anningsley Stingo (the breed's second Dual Ch.) out of Anningsley Dawn. This bitch proved to be a very successful foundation for the 'of Yeo ' kennel. Mrs Sawtell produced her first Champion, Ch. Masterpiece of Yeo, who was born in 1942. Many Yeo Champions were to follow in the UK and overseas in the six decades through to the 1990s. Miss Joan Gill obtained her first Golden Retriever in 1936, namely Simon of Brookshill. All present-day Westleys are descendants of his daughter, Westley Frolic of Yelme.

POST-WAR ERA

There was very little activity on the dog scene during the Second World War. There were no field trials or Championship shows held during this period, which resulted in a total lack of new title holders. Following the cessation of the war, normality gradually returned to the world of dogs both in the field and the show ring. The Golden Retriever Club resumed its activities by holding its first post-war Championship show in 1946. In the same year two new breed clubs were formed: the Golden Retriever Club of Scotland and the Northern Golden Retriever Club.

As a result of the lack of

Ch. Boltby Moonraker, pictured in 1952.

activity during World War Two, the quality of the breed diminished during this post-war era. This was due to both a high demand for puppies together with some indiscriminate breeding, purely to make money. The lack of quality was also due to shows being suspended, which meant that newcomers to the breed did not really know what a quality Golden Retriever should look like.

At this time, there was more activity and success in the field. The breed's first Dual Champion bitch, Noranby Destiny, was born in 1943. She gained her title in 1950 in the ownership of Mrs Charlesworth. Mr F.D. Jessamy's Stubblesdown Golden Lass was

born in 1944 and sold to Mr W.E. Hickmott. She went on to gain her Dual Champion title – the second bitch to do so. Joan Tudor's foundation bitch, Golden Camrose Tess, was born in 1946, bred by Miss Caddick. Tess was a litter sister to Mrs Stonex's Ch. Dorcas Glorious of Slat, sired by Sherrydan Damson out of Sunshine of Slat.

WINNERS IN THE 1950s
A number of influential show dogs appeared in the 1950s, including Mrs Lottie Pilkington's Ch. Alresford Advertiser. In his illustrious career, Advertiser won 35 CCs, many awards at field trials, plus the Crufts Gold Trophy. He also produced many

show-winning progeny. Ch. Boltby Skylon, owned by Mrs R. Harrison, won 29 CCs together with the honour of being twice Best of Breed at Crufts. Joan Gill's Ch. Simon of Westley won 21 CCs, many field trial awards, and the Crufts Gold Trophy five times. Miss Gill's Ch. Camrose Nicholas of Westley, bred by Joan Tudor, won 20 CCs, many field trial awards and a Best in Show at an All-Breed Championship Show. He also won the Crufts Gold Trophy. Int. Dual Ch. David of Westley was born in 1951, bred by Miss L. Ross, and campaigned in the show ring by his owner, Joan Gill. He won four CCs, and eight Green Stars (the Irish equivalent to Challenge

Certificates). David was handled in the field by his trainer, Jim Cranston, where he achieved 24 field trial awards, including a Diploma in the Retriever Championships. He gained his title in 1956 and has remained the only International Dual Champion Golden Retriever to this day.

KENNELS IN THE 1960-1970s

Many outstanding, influential dogs came to the fore in the 1960s. The first one deserving a mention is Ch. Camrose Tallyrand of Anbria, winner of 16 CCs and the sire of Ch. Camrose Cabus Christopher. Val Birkin started her Sansue kennel, which was to have a lasting influence on the breed with so many top-winning dogs over many years, including Ch. Sansue Camrose Phoenix and Ch. Sansue Golden Ruler. The Bryanstown kennel, owned by Mr and Mrs M. Twist and founded in 1941, achieved high honours in both Ireland and the UK over many years. Two of their outstanding dogs were Ch. & Ir. Ch. Bryanstown Gale Warning and Ch. Bryanstown Gaucho. Gaucho was a son of Ch. Stolford Happy Lad.

The 1970s were especially exciting years for the breed with many quality dogs making their mark in the show ring and in the field, and excelling in breed quality. We have to thank Joan Tudor for much of the improvement in quality in that era. There was a marked difference in type, making the Golden more attractive and with more substance, and much of this change emanated from the Camrose kennel.

The Westley kennel, founded

THE BREED'S TOP SIRE

The top-winning Golden Retriever, Ch. Camrose Cabus Christopher, remains, without doubt, the most influential sire in the breed. He has sired more Champions than any other Golden, he was the breed CC record holder for many years with 41 CCs to his credit, and he remains the only Golden Retriever to have twice won Best in Show at an all-breed Championship show.

Ch. Camrose Cabus Christopher: A prolific winner, and the breed's most influential sire.

in 1936 by Joan Gill, was joined in partnership in the early 1970s with Mervyn and Daphne Philpott. The early success of Miss Gill continued, with the kennel winning top honours in the show ring and in the field over a period of six decades. Miss Gill,together with Mervyn and Daphne Philpott, also owned the Standerwick affix, and won much acclaim in the field and in the show ring. Ch. Westley Victoria, owned by Mervyn Philpott and bred by Miss Gill and Mrs Philpott, deserves a mention as the most prolific brood bitch of the era. She was the dam of eight UK title holders, plus one in Ireland, and is behind so many of the top-winning Goldens in the ring today.

Ch. Simon of Westley: A fine representative from this outstanding kennel, winner of 21 Challenge Certificates.

The Camrose kennel continued to influence the breed not only in the UK but also throughout the world. Ch. Camrose Fabius Tarquin and Ch. Styal Stephanie of Camrose dominated the show ring throughout the late seventies and early eighties. Both Tarquin and Stephanie were sired by Ch. Camrose Cabus Christopher out of Ch. Styal Sibella. Ch. Styal Stephanie still holds the record for the most CCs won by a Golden Retriever bitch – 27 CCs and 19 Reserve CCs.

The Glennessa kennel, owned by Wing Cmdr. and Mrs Iles, produced many beautiful Goldens including many Champions. Arguably, the most outstanding dog from this kennel was Glennessa Escapade. He was the sire of Ch. Gaineda Consolidator of Sansue, Sh. Ch. Lost Heritage of Tarnbrook, Ch. Glenrose Fidelity, and Finnish & Est. Ch. Bridgefarm Glenleven. The Styal kennel, owned by Hazel Hinks, was based predominantly on Camrose breeding and produced a considerable number of top-quality Goldens over many years.

WEST COUNTRY SUCCESS

There were a number of very influential breeders in the West Country and ranking very highly was the kennel of Mrs S. Crick with the Moorquest affix. Mrs Crick bred or owned a number of Champions over three decades, including Ch. Moorquest Mugwump, Ch. Meant To Be at Moorquest, Ch. Make Haste to Moorquest and Mrs Beauchamp's Sh. Ch. Moorquest Minervois of Bolberry. Another prominent West Country sire to make a huge impression on the breed was Mrs Hilary Lambshead's Muskan Most Likely, known as Cloud. Although Cloud did not gain Championship status, he did sire many sound, well-constructed Goldens and his name still appears on many of the top-winning dogs' pedigrees in the show ring today. Mrs Lambshead campaigned two lovely bitches to their titles, Sh. Ch. Hingstondown Notoriety of Muskan and Sh. Ch. Muskan Miss Dior (by Ch. Moorquest Mugwump out of Sh. Ch. Hingstondown Notoriety of Muskan).

OUTSTANDING GOLDENS

Ch. Styal Scott of Glengilde was born in 1978, bred by Mrs Hinks and owned by Mr R. Scholes. Scott's sire was Ch. Nortonwood Faunus (sired by Ch. Camrose Cabus Christopher), and his dam was Ch. Styal Susila. Scott remains the breed CC record holder with 42 CCs, 29 Best of Breed and 23 Reserve CCs. He was the sire of seven UK Champions or Show Champions.

Another outstanding dog, and one of the all-time favourites, is Ch. Brensham Audacity, owned and bred, in 1976, by Mrs M. Wood. Harry won 19 CCs, 17 Best of Breed, four Gundog Groups and two Reserve Best in Shows at all-breed Championship shows. The highlight of his show career was winning the CC under Peggy Robertson (Stolford) at Crufts, and going on to win the Group under Mrs R. Parsons. He won his last CC and BOB in 1986 from the Veteran Class.

Ch. Nortonwood Faunus: Sire of 19 UK title holders.

INTO THE 1990s

The top-winning Golden Retriever dog of 1991 was the Shortmans' Sh. Ch. Rusway Sonnie Jim at Bridgefarm. Sonnie's dam was Bridgefarm Angelina of Rusway and he was sired by Mrs Crick's Ch. Moorquest Mugwump. Sonnie, born in 1986 and bred by Mr and Mrs R. Harding, won 11 CCs, all with Best of Breed, seven Reserve CCs and five Best in Shows at various Golden Retriever breed club Championship shows. He was the sire of Dovedown Royal Sovereign of Bridgefarm JW who, in turn, was the sire of Mrs Sawtell's Sh. Ch. Yeo Gold Medallion out of Yeo Lucky Star.

Sh. Ch. Yeo Gold Medallion (Monty) was born in July 1992 and was the last of Mrs Sawtell's long line of Golden Retriever Champions spanning half a century. Mrs Sawtell is currently the President of the South Western Golden Retriever Club and, at 92 years of age, still attends most club shows.

Throughout the nineties and into the new millennium, the Stanroph kennel, under the ownership and expertise of Anne Woodcock, has deservedly been at the top, with many Champions, CC and Junior Warrant winners in the UK and with much influence on the breeding and showing of Golden Retrievers overseas. Anne has earned the accolade of being the Top Breeder (Dog World/Pedigree) in the UK for some 11 years with a number of top stud dog and top brood bitch awards to her credit.

A-Z OF GOLDEN KENNELS

There are so many kennels that came to prominence throughout the 1970s, 1980s and 1990s. They include the following: Amirene (Mrs M. Woods), Bridgefarm (Mr and Mrs M. Shortman), Carasan (Mr B. Bargh), Catcombe (Mr and Mrs D. Andrews), Chinnordale (Mr and Mrs R. Maynard), Colbar (Mrs B. Keighley), Darthill (Cheryl Bawden), Davern (Mr and Mrs C. Lowe), Gatchells (Mrs B. Cowan and Mr and Mrs D. Mannings), Glenrose (Mr and Mrs G. Older), Linchael (Mrs L. Anderson), Lorinford (Mrs M. Everett-Monks), Mossburn (Mrs S. Pounds-Longhurst), Okus (Mrs C. Gilbert), Pinecrest (Mr and Mrs D. Balaam), Purbarn (Mrs J. Frankland-Mace), Rayleas (Mr and Mrs S. Zingg), Ritzilyn (Mr and Mrs G. Hennessy), Sandusky (Mrs Heather Morris), Sansue (Mrs V. Birkin), Sinnhein (Mr and Mrs J. Clark), Starlance (Mrs P. Bevis), Steval (Mrs V. Tregaskis), Tamarley (Mr and Mrs M. Watkins), Teecon (Mr and Mrs J. Tiranti) and Tugwood (Mr and Mrs A. Axe).

Sh. Ch. Rusway Sonnie Jim at Bridgefarm: Winner of 11 Challenge Certificates.

Top-winning male: Ch. Catcombe Corblimey.

Photo: Lynn Kipps.

THE CURRENT SCENE

The show scene has changed recently, as there are many Golden exhibitors coming to Championship shows in the UK from overseas, mainly from the European countries. There are also a number of UK exhibitors that enjoy showing their Goldens throughout Europe, and many UK judges are invited to award top honours overseas on a regular basis. This situation is good for competition and is good for the future of the breed as a whole, as it has tended to open up an extended gene pool for both the British and European breeders. Travel today between the UK and European countries is so much easier thanks to the PETS 'pet passport' scheme.

Some countries (e.g. France and Germany) did experience a problem with both type and temperament in the Golden due, in the main, to their too stringent health and temperament tests at the cost of all else. However, the overall standard of Golden Retrievers overseas has improved immensely during the past 20 years, and the European dogs are now coming to high-profile shows in the UK and winning top honours.

Sol, one of the earliest American imports, pictured with Archie Marjoribanks.

Bottom left and right: Am. Can. Ch. Speedwell Pluto: The first Golden Retriever to gain his title in the USA.

GOLDENS IN THE USA

According to the archives of the Golden Retriever Club of America (GRCA), it is widely accepted that the first Golden Retriever bitch to be recognised in the United States was 'Lady', belonging to the Honourable Archie Marjoribanks, the youngest son of the first Lord Tweedmouth. There is a photograph in the archival files of the GRCA depicting Archie Marjoribanks astride a horse with Lady sitting beside him. The photograph was taken at the Rocking Chair Ranch, Collinsworth County, Texas, in the early 1890s, which was owned and managed by Archie Marjoribanks. He had left the UK for America, taking with him a Golden Retriever male named Sol (sired by Sweep out of Zoe and born in 1882) who appears in Lord Tweedmouth's stud book in the early 1880s. It is possible, although with very little evidence to support it, that Sol may be the sire of Lady – out of a dam also taken to the States by Archie Marjoribanks. There is very little further information of relevance in the records of Golden Retrievers in North America until the turn of the century.

A GREAT PRODUCER

Adam with much influence on working dogs was Gilnockie Coquette. She was born in 1938 and owned by Ralph Boalt (brother-in-law of Col. Magoffin). Although Coquette did not win any titles in the field or on the bench, she produced, to three different sires, two Dual Champions, two Field Champions and four Show Champions.

Her progeny included Dual Champion Stilrovin Nitro Express, Field Champion Stilrovin Super Speed and Field Champion Stilrovin Katherine – all from the same litter sired by Stilrovin Bullet.

DEVELOPING THE GOLDEN RETRIEVER IN THE USA

The Golden Retriever Noranby Eventide was imported into Canada in the early 1920s and made up to Champion by Mr Bart Armstrong (Gilnockie). The breed then was not recognised as a Golden Retriever but Retriever (Wavy-Coated) by the Canadian Kennel Club. The first breed registration in the United States is recorded in late 1925. The dog was Lomberdale Blondin, an English import born in August 1922 out of Brandy and sired by Lomberdale Duke and owned by Robert Appleton. The breeder in the UK was Captain C. Waterhouse.

Interest in the breed really began to grow in Canada in 1930 with the import of Speedwell Pluto (Ch. Michael of Moreton x Sh. Ch. Speedwell Emerald) by Col. Samuel Magoffin. Pluto was bred in the UK by Mrs K. Evers-Swindell in 1929. Pluto was the foundation sire of the famous Rockhaven kennels in North Vancouver and the first Golden Retriever to become a bench Champion in the United States in 1932. He was also Best in Show at Puget Sound, Washington, in 1933. Speedwell Pluto became both a Canadian and an American Champion.

Although Golden Retrievers were recognised and accepted as a breed by the Canadian Kennel Club in 1927, it was some years later, in 1932, that the Golden Retriever was accepted as a breed by the American Kennel Club. This action followed a presentation by Bart Armstrong of the Gilnockie Kennel, Winnipeg,

Manitoba. Mr Armstrong sought much guidance concerning size and weight from Mrs W. M. Charlesworth of the Noranby kennel in the UK in his quest to get recognition for the breed. When Mr Armstrong died in 1932, Col. Magoffin took over the Gilnockie kennel organisation and ran it in conjunction with his own Rockhaven kennel.

INFLUENTIAL KENNELS

The Golden Retriever slowly gained popularity in the Central American States and kennels grew in prominence. Ralph Boalt, a brother-in-law of Colonel Magoffin, owned the Stilrovin kennel in Minnesota, and produced many top winners with awards in both the field and on the bench. The first national Field Trial Champion was King Midas of Woodend, who won the award in 1941.

Many kennels came to the fore in the late 1930s and into the early 1940s throughout the central states, with a few kennels being established on the east and west coasts. It was in the 1950s that Golden registrations gradually started to increase until it achieved startling numbers in the 1970s where the breed was winning regularly at all-breed Championship shows and in the obedience ring. However, through the 1940s, 1950s and 1960s many influential kennels came to prominence all over North America and Canada. Many pre-war kennels, including the aforementioned Rockhaven, Stilrovin and Gilnockie, plus

A highly successful dog in the show ring, 'Coach' (Ch.Happy HR Highmark Bad News Bears JH, SDHF) has won multiple Golden Retriever Specialities and Sporting Groups. He also shows great drive in the field, and has gained his Junior Hunter title.

Goldwood (Henry Christian and his daughter, Peggy Hilton), Whitebridge (John Wallace), Audlon (Mr & Mrs Mahlon Wallace), Woodend (Harold Ward), Oakcreek (Charles Snell), and Blue Leander (Peter Jackson), all had a huge influence on the establishment of the Golden Retriever in North America and Canada.

After the war, many new kennels shared success both in the show ring and in the field. It was in the 1950s that Golden registrations gradually started to increase until they achieved startling numbers in the 1970s, where the breed was winning regularly at all-breed Championship shows and in the obedience ring.

BREED ENTHUSIASTS

Everyone in the breed will accept, with gratitude, the fact that there are two US enthusiasts that deserve worldwide appreciation for their input of research, knowledge and experience into the breeding of Golden Retrievers. Firstly, Marcia Schlehr, for her decades of writing that have educated breeders in so many countries whilst sharing her own experiences from her 'Kyrie' kennel in Michigan. Mrs Schlehr is appreciated worldwide for her valuable input into the history of the breed.

Secondly, the Featherquest kennel on the East Coast of America is renowned among Golden Retriever devotees on both sides of the Atlantic as the home of Rachel Page-Elliott. Mrs Page-Elliott is well known for her pioneering research into analysing canine structure and movement, which led to her valued books and video publications on the subject. Her works are a 'must' for all Golden owners, breeders and judges alike.

There remains a marked difference in the general type of Golden Retriever from the UK type to its brothers and sisters in America. The US Golden still tends to be more versatile than the British Golden, with more competition in the field, in obedience and in agility.

A CHANGING BREED

Noranby Campfire:
The first Champion
in the breed.

A typical Golden Retriever
today. Note the angulation
front and rear, compared
with Noranby Campfire.

A NEW LOOK

When studying the history of the Golden Retriever, a general observation does show that the Goldens differ visually. The original 'type' of the Golden Retriever in the UK has changed gradually since the days of Mrs Charlesworth and the other pioneer breeders and exhibitors. The dogs of the 1920s tended to be taller, narrower in the head, less angulated and with a darker golden coat. They tended, as a breed, to work more than the Golden Retrievers of today, but as the years have passed, fashion has had an input into the style of Golden required by many owners and exhibitors.

The Goldens of today in the UK tend to be shorter in the leg with more angulation at both the front and rear, a more masculine (though not coarse) head and, certainly, the trend has gone toward a much lighter golden to cream coat. This is not a criticism, and there are exceptions to this viewpoint; it is merely a reflection from both in the ring and from the ringside. You only have to compare photographs of Ch. Noranby Campfire (pictured left) with a current Champion to see this point so well illustrated. We, as breeders and exhibitors, should expect some changes as the breed develops over the years, but should we say, "Stop, this is enough", or are we happy with the direction in which we are going and the progress of the breed in general?

It is often stated that many of the Golden Retrievers in the show ring today are not capable of a hard day's work. Is this due to a lack of stamina, their lack of working ability, or an element of both factors? The point is often raised that there are two types of Golden Retriever: the working type and the show type, and that certain points of the UK Kennel Club Breed Standard are being ignored. It is a common belief that both factions may be guilty, to some extent, of misinterpreting the Standard. Both should, ideally, work toward a show dog and a working dog looking similar in type, in overall structure and in conformation.

There are exceptions to this comment, and some good-looking dogs do work well. However, it is generally believed that we are still a long way from working and exhibiting Dual Champions on a regular basis. This takes me back to my earlier comment that Golden Retrievers in North America, generally, are worked more than their UK counterparts irrespective of whether they are shown. The dogs in the US still retain some of the original looks of the older type UK Golden Retriever, although they are gradually becoming closer as the US looks for more glamour and breeding traits change.

A GOLDEN RETRIEVER FOR YOUR LIFESTYLE

Chapter 3

The decision to purchase a Golden Retriever puppy should never be taken lightly; it is a huge commitment, and one that requires discussion with all members of the family that will be involved in the pup's care, exercise and feeding schedule. The addition of the 'little person' will have some effect on everyone in the household, and will upset many existing routines. It is also important to bear in mind that owning a Golden Retriever will change your lifestyle for some 12 years or so, which is the average lifespan of a Golden, although some live to 14 years and beyond. The Golden Retriever is a special dog. He will combine the virtues of glamour, intelligence and sincerity into one loyal, loving friend. A Golden does, however, tend to remain a puppy at heart, and will continue to be playful throughout his life. He will thrive on love and attention, together with his own collection of toys and playthings.

THE PROS AND CONS

The family, as a team, must discuss all aspects of their current lifestyle and every member must agree, wholeheartedly, that they are prepared for change and will puppy-walk whatever the weather and puppy-sit whenever necessary. Your new puppy, when mature, will have a glamorous golden coat that will need daily grooming. He or she will moult once or twice a year and leave his unwanted coat on carpets and furniture. Central heating does not help in this matter, causing more frequent shedding of hair throughout the wintertime. The Golden Retriever is also a comparatively large breed, and, due to his working origins, likes to pick up and carry objects in his mouth. This may be shoes, slippers, children's toys or even car keys, so early training is vital to ensure your puppy knows what he is allowed to play with, and what is definitely not to be touched.

Outside of the house, you will need to take special precautions, especially in the parts of the garden that will be accessible to your new Golden. So many of the plants we take for granted are poisonous to dogs and must be avoided. Another consideration is the family car. Is it big enough to accommodate a large dog together with all the family luggage and equipment, or will it need changing for an estate car or hatchback model? This is obviously a very serious financial consideration when added to all the forthcoming expenses. If, as a family, you cannot agree on these very important issues, or you are not in a financial situation that

Golden Retriever puppies are irresistible – but they are also very demanding.

will allow such expenditure, then a Golden Retriever puppy is certainly not for you. However, we will assume you have given the subject due discussion and consideration and have decided to proceed. What do you need to do next?

CAN YOU COPE WITH A PUPPY?

Many breeders will not sell puppies to families that are out at work each day, as a small puppy does need a lot of attention. Recruiting a friend or close family member to come in every hour or two to let the puppy into the garden for his toilet duty is not enough. Puppies need almost constant companionship, continual training and lots of affection.

This is not to say that pups can never be left alone. We all know this is impractical – there is shopping to do, children to take to school, and visits to the doctor and to the hairdresser, but the puppy must come first, particularly in his formative months. A puppy left alone for long periods will become very bored and will resort to chewing doors and furniture, removing wallpaper, chewing carpets, and will lack the necessary house training. This lack of attention will not make him a bad dog; his bad behaviour is due to poor education by his owners.

So we therefore assume one partner does not work, or the work pattern allows someone to be with the puppy most of the time. There may also be a need to draw up a family rota system as the puppy gets older, to decide who will have the responsibility for short walks and puppy-sitting duties. This needs to be prioritised prior to purchasing your pup, so everyone in the family is aware of where their personal responsibilities start and end. Adults and children alike need to be involved, as your Golden will rapidly become a close family member and will rely on everyone for love and support.

GREAT EXPECTATIONS

The next step is to decide what you, as a family, require from your Golden. Do you want just a very well behaved and loyal companion, or do you also want to show your dog? Do you want to compete in obedience or agility, or do you want to work your Golden in the field? The Golden Retriever is, traditionally, a working dog and does enjoy the opportunity to show his inbred skills in the field, whether it is just for fun or competing in the more serious working side. This can be picking-up on a local shoot, working tests or, if really keen and talented, you can compete in field trials. However, this type of competition is highly specialised, and dogs need to be specially bred and trained for the task. Handlers also need to undergo expert and prolonged training. Competing in field trials is not recommended for the beginner or the inexperienced, as it will take many years of hard work and a lot of hands-on

FINANCIAL IMPLICATIONS

Buying a Golden Retriever is a major commitment and will not only take a lot of your time, but will also cost a considerable amount of money. You have to buy a puppy, feed a puppy, pay for his course of vaccinations and, of course, find money to finance the initial outlay for all the necessary equipment needed for the home and car. It is all quite expensive. You also have to decide holiday arrangements: do you take puppy or do you use boarding kennels? Do you ask family to care for puppy, or will you employ the services of a house sitter? Boarding kennels and house sitters can become costly, particularly if you are away for extended holidays a couple of times each year.

Do you want a well-behaved companion dog, or do you have ambitions to work or compete with your Golden?

experience before anyone could ever consider participating in this standard of gundog work.

You must decide what 'type' of Golden you, as a family, require. There is a definite variation of type within the breed according to the bloodlines on the dog's pedigree; this should be well researched if you have a particular preference.

MALE OR FEMALE?

You also need to decide between a male or female puppy – both have their advantages together with a few lesser disadvantages. A male Golden is larger than a female and is usually more boisterous and outgoing, but he does not have a season to contend with every six months or so. The female, being smaller, may be more suitable for your particular environment, but you do have to be very mindful of male dogs when she is in season. At such times, it is important to ensure that she is not allowed to mix with other dogs while on walks, and that your garden is dog-proof to prevent any keen male dog from entering it and causing you

The male Golden Retriever (left) is bigger than the female, and may be more of a handful, particularly when he is growing up.

an unwanted cross-bred litter. Dependent on your location, you may have to restrict her to a secure garden for the three weeks' duration of her season.

The option is to neuter (spay) your Golden Retriever, assuming you have no intention of breeding. This will prevent further seasons and will, of course, ensure that she will not be able to have pups in the future. A lot of thought is necessary before making this decision as, once the operation has taken place, it is irreversible. There is also a tendency for a

bitch to gain weight and lose the lovely texture of the Golden's coat following spaying; all things, including a strict diet, must be considered.

A male Golden may be neutered (castrated) on your veterinary surgeon's advice if you are experiencing behaviour which indicates he may oversexed. Neutering generally has no effect upon the temperament of the Golden other than, in some cases, making them a little lazy and lethargic.

COAT AND COLOUR

When choosing a puppy, you need to be aware that there is a variation in the permitted shades of golden. "Any shade of gold or cream" is allowed by the UK Kennel Club Breed Standard, whereas the AKC Standard states: "Rich, lustrous golden of various shades." The choice is yours, and you may have a preference. It is worth bearing in mind that, at this stage, the colour of puppy's ears give an indication to his eventual shade of golden.

Coat types do vary among Goldens. Some lines produce quite flat coats while others have a wavier coat. Both types are correct according to the Breed Standard.

If a bitch is spayed (right) it will change the texture of her coat.

The Golden Retriever can have a flat coat (left) or a wavy coat, and the colour can range from cream to rich golden.

It is most important for the Golden to have a dense, waterproof undercoat to protect him from the water and cold weather he would experience while working. Golden coats do require some care and attention both in brushing, shampooing and trimming.

If you want to see the full range of shades and the different coat types, go to a local dog show as a visitor and see what you prefer. Talk to the exhibitors when they have completed their showing; they will be pleased to help and advise you.

FINDING A BREEDER

Whatever you decide in your proposed choice of dog or bitch, it is recommended that you join your local Golden Retriever club. You will find plenty of friendly, knowledgeable people – breeders, exhibitors and trainers – all willing to help and advise you and point you in the right direction of a reputable breeder. It is most important that you find an ethical Golden Retriever breeder and ensure that he or she is also a member of the Golden Retriever club in your area. You would be well advised to avoid

multi-breed kennels, or pet shops where all breeds are sold. This type of establishment often buys in litters of various breeds for selling on. In this situation, the dam will not be available for you to see, and the pups may have dubious pedigrees, as well as suspect temperaments and health. It is recommended that you check a kennel's credentials before committing yourself, ensuring you settle for a reputable and experienced breeder.

Finally, do not assume that the health and breeding of puppies is

KENNEL CLUB REFERRALS

National Kennel Clubs are also very helpful in helping you to find the pedigree puppy of your choice. The best plan is to go on the relevant website (see Appendices) to find out what litters have been bred in your area.

The UK Kennel Club will guide you in the direction of one of its 'accredited breeders'. This scheme is comparatively new; any breeder can join initially, but they must agree to adhere to the KC's codes of ethics. This code, among other issues, includes the need for health checks and the identification of all breeding stock by tattoo, microchip or DNA. The Kennel Club is aiming to raise the standard among breeders and to identify the less reliable people who breed for monetary gain. The Accredited Breeder Scheme awards accolades to breeders dependent upon their breeding experience, show achievements and membership of a breed club. This is certainly not a foolproof scheme, but it does go some way toward encouraging the genuine breeders.

Both the KC and AKC will give you contact details of a Golden Retriever club in your area, with some 13 UK clubs and 46 US representative clubs respectively, so it should not be difficult to find a reputable breeder.

of a high standard when you see 'Kennel Club registered' puppies advertised. This statement does not, in any way, guarantee that the dam and sire have been subjected to the recommended health schemes. Strangely, the UK Kennel Club will register litters irrespective of whether hip and eye tests have been carried out.

The local veterinary practice may be able to help you locate a reputable breeder, or you could look in one of the specialist weekly dog papers, such as *Dog World* or *Our Dogs*, that are available from all good newsagents. The important thing is to ensure that the breeder is a responsible person who is prepared to help and advise you, and for you to ensure that the breeder's home, kennels and whelping facilities are clean and hygienic.

VISITING A BREEDER

The breeder you eventually choose is most important, as this decision is the foundation of your Golden experience. Most breeders are very helpful and responsible people and will assist you even if they have no planned litter of their own. The breeder may suggest another option; they will have the pedigrees and the knowledge of the bitches that have visited their dogs, and will help you decide which direction to take.

Let us now assume that you have found a breeder who can help you. The first question to ask is: when is the litter due? This has important implications, as you want to ensure that the puppy is ready to come to his new home at a time when it is most convenient for you. Next, you should make an appointment and visit the breeder's premises well in advance of the puppy being available. Personally, we like to meet prospective puppy purchasers prior to the bitch being mated. We show them all our dogs, both male and female, to illustrate the difference in size and the variation in colour. Following this, they are then

The aim of a good breeder is to produce a line of sound animals that are typical of the breed.

taken on a tour of the whelping room where the pups will be born and raised.

You will want further information on the health schemes to which both the dam and sire should be certificated. There are a number of schemes for Golden Retrievers, including hip scoring, eye checking, elbow scoring and heart checks. The first two are by far the most important: the hip results must be within acceptable parameters, and all eye checks must be certified clear.

It is vitally important that all breeding stock undergo these checks for the future good of the breed. Ensure that you ask to see current copies of the hip and eye certificates; if you are not too clear on their content, make a few notes to discuss with your veterinary practitioner later. No genuine breeder would object. There are also heart checks and elbow X-rays, which are not mandatory, but are left to the breeder's discretion.

Some breeders have their litter of puppies either tattooed or microchipped prior to going to their new homes, although we prefer to have a pup microchipped at the time of his first vaccinations. If the breeder has chosen to have the pups tattooed or microchipped, then the relevant paperwork will be included when you collect your puppy.

EYE CHECKS

Golden Retriever eye checks are under the auspices of the British Veterinary Association and the Kennel Club in the UK. The eyes are examined annually for hereditary diseases associated with the Golden Retriever. The offending eye diseases are currently: multifocal retinal dysplasia (MRD), generalised and central progressive retinal atrophy (GPRA and CPRA) and hereditary cataract (HD).

Golden Retriever eye examinations must be carried out by a KC/BVA-approved canine ophthalmic specialist. There are more than 30 eye experts in practice throughout the UK. They are approved by the BVA and are

HIP-SCORING SCHEMES

Both the UK Kennel Club and the American Kennel Club promote the use of the hip schemes and, although they do differ slightly, the aims are the same and the end results are very similar.

In the UK, the hip-scoring scheme involves the dog having both hips X-rayed by a veterinary radiologist, and the plates are submitted to the British Veterinary Association for scoring. Each hip is scored on nine specific areas of construction and scored between 1 and 53 – the lower the score, the better the hip formation. The best hip score, therefore, would be 0:0 and the worst scenario 53:53. Currently, the average score for the Golden Retriever is a total of 18.43 (Malcolm Willis 2006), so you should endeavour to find a dam and sire with total scores in the 20s or lower. (Allowing for the quality of temperament, eyes, and type to be factored in).

In the US, the hip scheme is run under the auspices of the Orthopaedic Foundation for Animals (OFA). Each dog's X-ray plate is subject to scrutiny by a panel of three veterinary radiologists, and if all three agree that the animal is free of dysplasia then a certificate and identification number will be issued. However, if there is some degree of dysplasia present, the plates will be rated 'mild', 'moderate' or 'severe', with neither a certificate nor identification number being issued.

The minimum age for X-raying and assessing is 12 months old in the UK and 24 months old in the US. Any X-rays produced prior to 12 months of age in the UK cannot be submitted to the BVA. In the US, any submission prior to 24 months of age will receive a temporary assessment and it will be necessary for the dog to be X-rayed and assessed again at the required 24 months.

Researchers agree that hip dysplasia involves a polygenic trait – i.e. several inherited genetic factors contribute to the condition. However, they do not ignore the fact that environmental pressures may also influence the problem to a great extent. (For more information on hip dysplasia, see Chapter 8.)

It is vital that all breeding stock is hip scored.

members of the BVA specialist panel. Incidents of eye problems have lessened over recent years as a result of the aforementioned tests.

The eye-testing procedure in the United States is very similar to that in the UK. The US test data is submitted to the Canine Eye Registration Foundation (CERF), which will, if there is no evidence of a problem, issue a clear eye certificate. The eyes are required to be checked annually in the US as in the UK. (For more information on inherited eye conditions, see Chapter 8.)

TYPE AND TEMPERAMENT

We must never lose sight of the fact that temperament is by far the most important asset in the Golden Retriever, and this must not be lost under any circumstances. As an illustration, it was evident in a couple of European countries that breeders had tended to put too high an importance on hip scores at the expense of type and temperament. These two points are the major components of the Golden Retriever and must not be lost.

I will admit, however, that during my recent judging appointments throughout Europe, I have noticed a general improvement in the 'type' and the quality of the Golden Retrievers bred in these countries now. They are coming close to matching the standard of the top dogs in the UK.

Breeding for the Golden Retriever's temperament is a top priority.

HEALTH ALERT

I would like to add one point on the subject of the Golden's health. As the coefficient of breeding increases (the coefficient of breeding highlights closer inbreeding between Goldens), the incidence of lymphoma, or lymphosarcoma, also appears to increase. It is open to speculation whether the two issues are linked in any way or if it is purely coincidental. It may be prudent for you to enquire if your chosen breeder has had any major problems with cancer in their Golden Retrievers over recent years, as this can often have very serious consequences and can lead to much heartbreak at a very early age.

REARING PUPPIES

Now that you are satisfied with the health checks of your proposed puppy's parents, the next question is to ask where the puppies will be reared. All reputable breeders will be happy to give you a short tour and explain their nursery set-up to you. Select a breeder whose puppies are reared, preferably, in a home environment – not in ill-equipped outside kennels. Puppies reared in a home environment will be used to family visits, the noise of the television, radio, vacuum cleaner and washing machine. This will ensure that your new puppy is in a well-prepared condition when he eventually arrives home with you.

Do not be afraid to ask questions. Ask to see the dam, and any other homebred stock on the premises, and check to see if the facilities are clean and hygienic. Ask about longevity: the average lifespan of the breeder's particular lines. At this stage, most breeders will show you photographs and pedigrees of their dogs, both current and past. This will give you a very good indication of what you might expect from your new addition when maturity approaches. You should also ask the purchase price and whether a deposit is required.

BOOKING A PUPPY

If you are satisfied with everything you have seen and

Ideally, the puppies will be reared in a home environment and will be well socialised.

heard, ask if your name can be added to the breeder's puppy list – the list of dogs and bitches already booked by other potential buyers. The breeder will tell you when the planned mating is due to take place, or when the pups are due if the mating has already occurred.

The breeder should also explain the reason for Kennel Club endorsements, if they choose to have them added to your puppy's registration documents. There are currently two endorsements that a breeder may add at the time of initial registration. Firstly, that 'progeny are not eligible for registration' and secondly, 'not eligible for the issue of an export pedigree'. Both endorsements act as some

protection for the future of the puppy, and to try to ensure that, if the pup is bred from, then it is done correctly. If, in the future, you would like your bitch to have a litter, you will need to discuss your plans with the breeder of your puppy, ensuring you have had the required health checks with satisfactory results and you have chosen a suitable partner for your Golden. If all criteria are met, the breeder can lift the endorsement by writing to the Kennel Club, and you are free to continue with your breeding plans.

If you have found a breeder with a litter already born and the pups are not previously reserved, beware, as most reputable breeder's litters are booked and

sold well before the mating takes place. Once the pups are born, the breeder usually notifies everyone on the waiting list of the date of birth and of how many puppies and of which sex. This is the crucial moment when you know if there is a puppy in the litter for you.

THE RIGHT CHOICE

We will assume that you have been informed that there is a puppy available for you. The selection of which pup goes to which home is best left to a later date when the puppies are established and forming their own little personalities. In the current age of computers and email, it is very easy to notify everyone of the good news

Make sure you see the mother with her puppies to get some idea of the temperament they are likely to inherit.

together with a 'first' photograph. We do this with a weekly update together with a photograph. This not only keeps everyone aware of what is happening and the progress being made, but it also cuts down on time and telephone calls.

The first visit to see the pups will be arranged when the litter is between three and four weeks of age. Prior to this, the pups do not move very much and their eyes have not yet opened. It is always essential to contact the breeder to make a firm appointment to view. Do be punctual, and do not outstay your allotted time, as another prospective purchaser may well be following on after your visit.

It is imperative that you ensure you have not been in contact with other animals prior to your visit, as the breeder will not want any potential infection passed to the puppies. You may be asked to remove your shoes and wash your hands. Please conform willingly, as the health of the babies is most important.

Then comes the time to choose your puppy. This is usually when the puppies are about seven to eight weeks of age, when they are fully weaned, wormed and totally independent of their mother. Please be patient and be led by your breeder's advice. If you have young children, the breeder may have noticed a particularly outgoing youngster that would fit in well with your family; likewise a quieter puppy may be better suited to an older couple who are looking for a companion. When viewing or collecting, it is important for you, the purchaser, to ensure that your puppy is lively and alert. Do not select the introvert puppy hiding in the corner. Shyness at this early stage could be indicative of an untypical Golden temperament. You must be sure that the puppy you finally choose is visually healthy and does not have a runny nose or eyes and is not pot-bellied. The latter could indicate the presence of worms.

A SHOW PUPPY

If you decide you would like to show your Golden, you would be well advised to take an experienced person with you to see the pups. You want an outgoing puppy that is not shy or frightened. Conformation wise, you would look for a puppy that is 'square', not long in the body or long in the leg, one with the correct bite (although this can be a little difficult at such an early age) and, if a male, that two testicles are evident. Check the topline; you want a continuous line across the back and on to the tail. Ensure the tail is neither low set nor carried high (a gay tail), as both are undesirable and would be penalised in the show ring. Look for good pigmentation around the eyes and on the pads. It is difficult to find a good show puppy without experience; go to an established breeder, look at the dogs and decide if you like what you see.

The best age to choose a puppy is when it is between seven and eight weeks of age.

PUPPY TO CHAMPION
The breeder will help you to assess show potential. This is Sh. Ch. Rusway Sonnie Jim photographed as he is growing up.

Sonnie Jim at seven weeks.

Sonnie Jim, now a Show Champion, pictured at two-and-a-half years old.

Best in Show winner, Sonnie Jim at Bridgefarm, aged three years.

If you are planning to work your Golden Retriever, you will need to go to a specialist breeder who produces dogs for the field.

A WORKING HOME

If you require a puppy for working, you should contact a breeder whose Goldens are from working lines. You will find them so much easier to train. However, you need a lot of instruction and training yourself to enable you to train a dog to competition standard, and it is advisable to ensure you are competent before embarking on a training programme for your dog. You need to decide whether a dog or a bitch would suit your requirements; take advice again. Bitches have seasons and it is most annoying if this coincides with the shooting season. Basic training should start very early at home, and then you will need to enlist the help of a specialist trainer who will help you to prepare your dog for gundog work.

TAKING ON A RESCUED DOG

You may feel that you would like to rehome a rescued dog. This is a very admirable plan, and one to be commended, as there are many Goldens in need of new, loving homes. The reasons for rehoming range from marriage break-ups to bereavement, from moving house to allergy problems. Over the years that my wife and I have been involved in rescue in the south-west of England, we have heard just about every excuse imaginable.

Sad situations sometimes arise due to uncaring breeders selling puppies to the wrong people, with no care for their future. But the most common reason for rehoming is when a family breaks up. This situation is heartbreaking for everyone concerned: the dog's owners, the rescue officer who must take the dog away, and, most particularly, the children who must lose the dog they love.

Goldens deserve a good home, with lots of love and affection, but if you decide to rehome a rescued dog, make sure you contact one of the many Golden Retriever club rescue officers for advice and assistance. You need to know the history of the dog, and find out why he is being offered for rehoming. You also need to discover if the dog is suffering from any ongoing health problems that could prove costly to you over a long period. Golden Retrievers are also available at all-breed rescue centres, and again, you must rely on the staff to give you a complete history of the dogs that are available for adoption.

There are rare instances where Golden Retrievers have shown aggression or even bitten their owners or family. This cannot be tolerated under any circumstances, and dogs with this problem should not be rehomed through the rescue organisations. Golden Retrievers that need rehoming are usually screened by rescue officers for inappropriate temperament or any health problems, so an aggressive dog or bitch should not be put up for adoption. Having made the point, I must emphasise that poor temperament is a rare occurrence, as the Golden Retriever is a very gentle and loving breed, but these adverse traits do occasionally appear.

A SUITABLE HOME

If you find the rescued dog you want, you must expect to be vetted prior to the 'adoption'.

The rescue officer's intention is to find a home where the family has sufficient time to devote to the new addition, and can afford to keep and feed him. Above all, a rescued Golden needs a loving, permanent home.

You will be asked many questions:

- Do you have children?
- Do you have other pets?
- Do you live in a house or a flat?
- Is your garden suitably fenced?

You may think this rather intrusive, but it is the rescue officer's duty to do his or her best to find a suitable home for the dog. A rescue officer has wide experience of rehoming, and his or her decision is usually correct. Most Golden Retrievers settle happily into their second home – and this time the home will last, hopefully, for the rest of their days.

THE PERFECT FAMILY DOG

Whatever avenue you choose in selecting your Golden Retriever puppy, please do not let distance be an obstacle to you. Be prepared to travel if necessary – a couple of trips of a 100 miles or so is more than worthwhile if you are finding a family companion who will be with you for a decade or more. You will also be forming a relationship with the puppy's breeder, which may prove important as your puppy grows and matures

The Golden Retriever is a family dog in every sense. Your Golden will become another child in the family, bringing you love and entertainment; he will share your happiness and excitement, and will ease your pain and disappointment – the Golden Retriever is certainly a breed to be treasured.

The Golden Retriever loves his family, and soon you will not be able to imagine life without one.

THE NEW ARRIVAL

Chapter 4

The time has come to collect your new Golden Retriever puppy. After months of planning, followed by weeks of visiting your new pup, the day has finally arrived. Do not make the mistake of being so excited about getting your puppy that you neglect essential preparations. It is important that you are well prepared for this new addition to the family.

IN THE GARDEN
First and foremost, make sure the garden is well fenced, and check to see that every little gap or hole is blocked up. It is quite amazing how a Golden Retriever puppy can find his way through fences and bushes. You will also need to check for any plants that could be poisonous (enquire at your local garden centre as to which plants are toxic, or do some research on the internet).

If you have a large garden, you may decide that it is a good idea to fence off part of it for your Golden's exclusive use. This will not only save the rest of your lawn and your plants, but it is also easier to keep an eye on your dog. Goldens are great diggers, and puppies in particular cannot resist chewing plants. So if you are a keen gardener, this may save a lot of heartbreak all round.

You may decide to make a

Golden Retriever puppies are great explorers, so make sure your home and garden are safe.

small run or play area that is fenced in, perhaps laying some paving slabs down to make a dry area for the puppy to play on if the weather is wet.

IN THE HOUSE

In the house it is very important to make an area for the puppy's bed or indoor kennel. Most people find an area in the kitchen or utility room, which is usually close to the back door and garden.

Decide in advance which rooms your puppy is allowed access to, and then you can make sure they are safe for an inquisitive puppy who will want to explore every nook and cranny. Potential hazards include trailing electric wires, houseplants, floor-length curtains, and fringes on furniture. The best plan is to look at each room from your puppy's perspective and work out what he may be able to reach.

If you want to restrict access to certain rooms, or you want to prevent your puppy going upstairs, you will need to fit baby gates, which can act as a temporary barrier. It is important that the puppy knows where he can and cannot go in the house from the moment he arrives home.

BUYING EQUIPMENT

You do not need to spend a fortune on doggy equipment, but there are a few essential purchases:

INDOOR KENNEL

You will find that an indoor kennel/crate is a wise investment, providing a safe, secure den for your Golden Retriever. It is advisable to buy a crate that is big enough to accommodate an adult Golden. The minimum size is 45 ins by 24 ins by 36 ins (120 by 90 by 60 cms). This may

look rather big for an eight-week-old puppy, but you can make it cosy by putting a cardboard box lined with bedding at the back of the crate. The best type of bedding to use is synthetic fleece, which is machine-washable and dries quickly. You can line the front of the crate floor with newspaper, which will assist with house training (see page 64).

There are many different types of indoor kennels on the market. A soft cage is a popular type; it folds down and can be used in the car if you wish. These cages are made of a strong, plastic material with mesh panels in the sides and top; they are light to carry and can be easily moved around the house. You can also buy metal crates, which many people prefer, as they cannot be chewed. This type of crate does fold down, but it is heavy to carry and not so easy to transport in the car.

If you locate an indoor kennel in the kitchen or utility room, your puppy will appreciate having another bed in the main living room.

PUPPY PEN

You may choose to purchase a puppy pen, sometimes known as an X-pen. This can be used in addition to an indoor kennel, at times when you are working in the kitchen, for example, but you do not want your puppy to be running loose. You can also use the puppy pen in the garden to make sure you pup does not stray too far and get into mischief.

DOG BED

Even if you are using an indoor kennel, you will still want a dog bed so your Golden Retriever has his own place to lie in your sitting room or study. I would always recommend a hard plastic bed, which can be easily washed out. Line the bed with fleecy bedding to make it warm and cosy.

FEEDING/WATER BOWLS

Stainless-steel feeding bowls are the best to purchase, as they are easy to clean and hard to destroy! You will also need a water bowl that is not too deep. Golden Retriever puppies love to play with water, so if you don't want to turn your kitchen floor into a swimming pool, buy a shallow bowl and do not overfill it.

COLLAR AND LEAD

When choosing a collar and lead, I recommend the nylon type, which is very strong and usually washable. The lead needs a secure fastening to attach to the collar. Never use a full chain

collar, as this will mark the coat and pull the fur out, as well as being too harsh for positive, reward-based training.

Make sure the collar is not too loose otherwise your puppy will free himself, which could have lethal consequences if you are in the street. You can alter the fitting, but the first collar you buy will not last long, as a Golden Retriever grows at a great

rate. You will probably need to purchase two or three collars over a 12-month period.

GROOMING GEAR

It is important to buy some grooming products so your puppy gets used to being groomed from an early age. I recommend stainless-steel combs and wire brushes, as, in time, you will find that your puppy's coat

Start grooming from an early age so that your puppy learns to accept all-over handling.

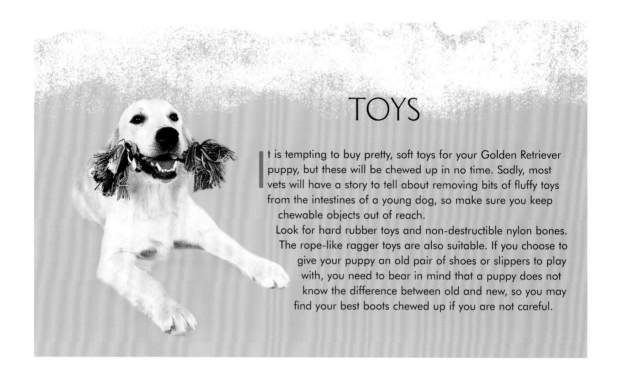

TOYS

t is tempting to buy pretty, soft toys for your Golden Retriever puppy, but these will be chewed up in no time. Sadly, most vets will have a story to tell about removing bits of fluffy toys from the intestines of a young dog, so make sure you keep chewable objects out of reach.

Look for hard rubber toys and non-destructible nylon bones. The rope-like ragger toys are also suitable. If you choose to give your puppy an old pair of shoes or slippers to play with, you need to bear in mind that a puppy does not know the difference between old and new, so you may find your best boots chewed up if you are not careful.

will be quite thick and will mat easily if you don't keep it brushed regularly. Grooming has dual benefits: not only does it keep your puppy's coat clean and shiny, it also gets him used to being handled, so he will enjoy grooming sessions when he is an adult.

It is also advisable to trim your puppy's claws regularly. Many older dogs do not like their nails being cut, so the younger you begin, the better. You can start by simply lifting the puppy's feet and making a game of it, giving a treat as a reward. I recommend the guillotine type of nail-clippers, which are the safest and the easiest to use.

COLLECTING YOUR PUPPY

Now it is time to collect your new, fluffy Golden Retriever puppy. Take plenty of towels with you, some kitchen roll, a bowl and a bottle of water. Not all puppies travel well on their first trip in the car, so you need to be prepared. I try not to feed my puppies too close to the time they are to travel, to reduce the chance of car sickness.

Take some toys and some bedding, so that you can make your puppy as comfortable as possible. It is important to remember that, for many puppies, the first experience of the car is when they leave the breeder's home. This can be a

stressful time for any puppy, so try to make it a happy and secure trip.

I always suggest my new owners sit with the puppy in the back of the car for this first trip to their new home; from then onwards, you must decide where you want your puppy to travel in the car. If you have an estate car or a hatchback, put a travel cage in the back of the vehicle, to keep the dog safe. If using the back seats of a car, a canine seat belt or harness should be used, to keep the dog secure.

Many dogs take a while to get used to the car, so take your puppy out on short, frequent trips to places he enjoys, such as the park or socialisation classes, so he learns to associate the car with enjoyable experiences. If your puppy continues to be car sick, try to avoid feeding him before the journey and seek advice from your vet for any suitable medication. It can become quite a habit with many dogs, if left untreated, so take steps while the pup is young to prevent this from happening.

Always remember to leave plenty of windows open in the car should you ever have to leave your puppy alone in the car for short periods, and always park in a shady position and leave a bowl of water down. Even with these measures, no dog should be left in a car in warm weather, as the car interior quickly heats up and the dog can die.

I always suggest that when new owners collect their new puppy, they bring along their children too. It is important that, in that first few hours of leaving the breeder, a new bond of friendship is made. You are the pup's new

After all the hard work of rearing the puppies, it is time for the breeder to say goodbye as they go to their new homes.

family now and so everyone must be part of the puppy's new life and journey to his new home.

PAPERWORK

Most breeders will supply you with a full pedigree of your puppy, a Kennel Club registration certificate, a complete diet sheet and starter pack, with enough food for the next few days. A puppy will normally leave the breeder at about eight weeks of age.

FOOD

Your puppy should be on four meals a day at this time, and it is a good idea to find out from the breeder what food they have been feeding the litter, so you can purchase a medium sack of food in advance. You may find that in the first few days of your puppy arriving home, he will probably go off the food you have been told to give him. Don't be tempted to change the diet at this stage; it is important that you stick with the food he has been used to. I always supply my new puppy owners with a full diet sheet, together with a few tips on how to overcome these problems.

It often helps to put a small amount of fish or tinned meat on the dry food after you have soaked it with a little warm water. If the pup just walks away from the food, pick it up and try it again later. Don't leave the food down. Puppies do get hungry eventually and will soon be asking for their dinner. As a last resort, to re-establish an appetite, try to offer some goats' milk, which puppies can digest more easily than cows' milk. If you

You may have to teach your puppy 'food manners' so that he is not over-protective about his bowl at mealtimes.

have problems with loose motions, then add a little live yoghurt or probiotic powder to the meals, to settle his tummy.

It is not uncommon for young puppies to show some form of defensive behaviour, such as growling or lifting their lip, when they are approached while feeding. This behaviour often occurs in the litter when the pups are competing for food. Such behaviour is not acceptable in the domestic environment and it is important that owners are able to walk past their dog while he is eating and retrieve food items from their mouths if the need arises. You need to teach your puppy that people approaching the food bowl are not threatening and therefore you should resist the temptation to keep taking his bowl away from him. Rather than proving to your

puppy that you are in control, you will simply teach him that you are a threat to his food source and that he should defend it from you at all cost. Instead, you should go through the routine of standing beside your puppy's bowl while he is eating, and repeatedly ask him to sit or wait while you add some more food to his bowl. This will increase your puppy's confidence about you being near his bowl. Once your puppy is happy to have you near his bowl, you can now extend the training by lifting the bowl up off the floor to add more food and then place it back on the ground for your puppy to continue eating.

HEALTH TREATMENTS
Your puppy should have been wormed at least three times before he leaves the litter, and it

is important to continue the worming programme on a regular basis for the rest of the puppy's life. Your vet will advise you on the products available. Make sure the breeder gives you details of what the puppy has been wormed with, and the dates.

Many breeders will offer you six weeks' free insurance, starting from the day you collect your puppy. Details should be given to you in your puppy pack.

As a breeder of Golden Retrievers, I very rarely inoculate my puppies before eight weeks, so most puppies leave us without inoculations. It is important to make sure your new puppy does not mix with other dogs (apart from your own older dog in your own home) until your vet has given the all-clear. Similarly, never be tempted to take your new puppy out into any public places, such as parks and local walks, until pup has had his complete course of injections and has adequate immunity.

When I send my puppies to their new homes, they have always had a bath and a flea treatment. Fleas and ticks can be quite a problem in the summer months especially, and it is important to check your puppy's coat when grooming for signs of flea dirt, which looks like little specks of dirt. Often your puppy will be scratching a lot if he has a problem with fleas.

For more information about fleas, ticks, worming and inoculations, see Chapter 8.

Arriving in a new home is a bewildering experience for a young puppy.

ARRIVING HOME

It is always a great event when a new puppy or older dog arrives, but integrating a puppy or older dog is not always that easy. The first few weeks of life together will set the pattern for your dog's behaviour in the years to come and will lay down the foundation for the relationship between you.

THE FIRST DAY

There are lots of lessons that puppies need to learn, and learning is most effective when it takes place in the context of positive interaction and reward. Therefore, training will involve praising the good behaviour rather than punishing the not so good.

Taking on a rescued dog can often be very rewarding, as very often you find that all they require is a little love and attention. However, it is generally harder to change the bad habits of the older dog. Established habits will require hard work and patience to undo them.

Not all rescued dogs have had a bad start in life; many are in need of a home due to a change in their owners' circumstances, meaning they can no longer look after a dog. Golden Retrievers are very adaptable, and they usually respond very well to a new home.

During the first day, your Golden Retriever needs plenty of time to get used to his new surroundings and it is important that you make the house rules now rather than later. Make sure you spend lots of time with him; show him the garden and where you intend him to sleep at night or during the day. If you are using an indoor pen or cage, then let him play in it freely. Golden Retriever puppies adjust very quickly to their new home and are usually very adventurous and happy to explore their surroundings.

All interactions with children should be supervised in the early stages, to get the relationship off on a good footing.

CHILD'S PLAY

If you have children in the family, then it is most important that they are always supervised with the puppy. Accidents can happen when the dog is very young; puppy teeth are like needles and can easily catch a child's face or hand in play, without the dog even realising what he has done. I find that all my Goldens love children and can't wait to see my granddaughter when she arrives. They adore her and all push in for her attention. She is only four years old and has complete control over all seven dogs. She has grown up with the puppies over the years and has complete respect for them, and they respect her, too.

It is most important that you have strict rules on how the children handle the puppy. Never let the children pick up the pup, as he may wriggle and be dropped. It also ensures that the puppy learns to see children as friendly playmates and enjoyable to be with.

Never allow the children to disturb the puppy while he is sleeping or eating, and never allow them to tease the puppy. Most Golden Retrievers form a lovely bond with children, so always start to socialise him with the children from a very early age.

Puppies tend to play with their mouths open – this is known as 'mouthing'. Golden Retrievers will often hold an arm or pull at your jumper, but it should be discouraged, as puppy teeth are very sharp and many children get quite upset by this.

MEETING OTHER PETS

When you are introducing a new puppy to the resident dog, or other pets in the family, it is important to do so gradually. An older dog or cat will not necessarily appreciate a youngster running amok, sleeping in their beds, or playing with their toys.

If you have a resident adult dog, allow him to meet the puppy in a controlled situation. The garden is generally the best place as the resident dog will not feel so protective. Supervise initial interactions, but try not to interfere too much, as the dogs will soon reach their own understanding. Do not leave the adult and puppy alone together to begin with, and then allow them short periods on their own once you are confident that good relations have been established.

It is also important to supervise mealtimes; a puppy may try to steal the adult dog's food, and this will inevitably lead to trouble. Make sure the two dogs are fed well apart from each other, and stay in the same room with them until they have both finished eating.

If you are careful in the initial stages, the two dogs will soon become the best of pals and will not need close supervision.

I have always kept Goldens and cats together, and they live together very happily. However, if you are introducing a new puppy to a resident cat, make sure you supervise all initial interactions – and make sure the cat is able to get away from the puppy when she chooses.

THE FIRST NIGHT

This time spent with your puppy is well worth it, as, come night time, he will be very alone and

If you are tactful to begin with, your resident dog will quickly accept the newcomer.

will probably not be too happy about being left. The first night is generally the worst; some puppies are fine and sleep with no problem, but some just don't give up. Try to be strong and not go to your puppy; he will sleep eventually, but it is not easy to hear him fret.

It may be helpful to leave a radio on in the room, so the pup

can hear some background noise. A soft toy for company helps, too. Leave some water down for him, but if he spends his time playing with it, then pick it up and only leave it down when you are around so you can tell him "no" and discourage him. Most puppies adjust to sleeping in their new bed very well, but some take a few nights to settle.

HOUSE TRAINING

Your next challenge will be house training your new puppy. Most new owners are prepared for a few accidents and a little more cleaning, but when house training is unsuccessful or takes a long time to establish, then the relationship between puppy and owner can be pushed to breaking point. The aim, therefore, is to establish reliable house training as soon as possible. By following a few simple rules it is possible to maximise your chances of success and make the whole process far less stressful for all.

It is important that your puppy understands where to relieve himself and learns to associate going outside with going to the toilet. There are certain times when it is most likely that your puppy will want a loo break, and you can increase your chances of successful house training by making sure your puppy is outside at the following times: when he first wakes up, after every meal, after drinking water and after playing.

Minimising the opportunities for accidents is important. If your pup has an accident inside the house, he will learn an inappropriate association (i.e. house and toilet, rather than garden and toilet).

Always remember to praise your puppy and to give a small reward when he gets it right, but try to do this outside so that he understands that it is a good thing to perform outdoors. Going to the toilet is a necessary and natural behaviour and any form of punishment while house training will lead to confusion.

Puppies tend to 'look guilty' if they are shouted at the scene of an accident, but this isn't guilt – it is a demonstration of appeasement, as the puppy wants you to stop being cross. Your puppy cannot associate his previous act of going to the toilet with the punishment he is receiving, and his behaviour is simply designed to deflect your anger. So threatening your puppy with a rolled-up newspaper, shouting at him, or, worse, rubbing his nose in it, are all cruel and unacceptable and should be avoided at all costs. House training is not easy, but stick to the rules and you will succeed.

If you take your puppy into the garden at regular intervals, he will soon understand what is required.

THE CRATE SOLUTION

Many owners anticipate some levels of destruction when they take on a new puppy, but using an indoor cage when you cannot supervise your Golden for short periods, will prevent this. If your puppy has the freedom of the home, then he may well chew items you'd prefer he didn't! If you do have to leave your puppy for a few hours, keep him safe in a crate of a puppy-proofed room, and leave him with some toys and hard nylon bones to play with. Most damage is usually caused in the early days when your puppy is teething and is more often because he is bored.

If your puppy or older dog continues to be destructive, then there may be a reason for his behaviour and a more in-depth investigation would be necessary. Potential causes include separation anxiety, frustration and boredom. Always resist the temptation to punish your dog when you find the damage. Obviously this can be very difficult when you come home to find your home in chaos, but the use of punishment after the event will only lead to confusion and run the risk of damaging your relationship with your puppy. Indoor crates can be used for adult dogs, but often, as your puppy grows up and learns to respect your home and belongings, then he will be able to have more freedom when you are not around.

You will need to introduce your puppy to his indoor kennel gradually. Set the crate up so that the puppy can wander in at will, and place some interesting toys and treats inside so that he starts to associate his crate as being an enjoyable place to be. Once he is happy to spend time in the crate, try shutting the door for a little while so that he gets used to it.

An indoor crate provides a safe, secure home for your puppy when you cannot supervise him.

HOUSE RULES

When it comes to the basic training of your puppy or older Golden Retriever, it is important for every member of the family to use the same approach. It is probably best to have a family meeting to decide on the commands that you are going to use and the house rules you are going to establish. Puppies need clear boundaries and inconsistency is probably the commonest cause of training problems.

Golden Retrievers always want to please and be part of the family; they are not hard to train, but you must be firm and everyone must stick to the rules laid down. If you don't wish for your puppy to go upstairs in the bedrooms, then don't let him. If the children sneak him upstairs without your knowledge and then, on another occasion, you catch him trying to climb the stairs, the poor, confused dog really won't understand what is going on. It is the same with the furniture. If you allow your puppy on the settee one day, then tell him off another day when he jumps up with muddy paws, he won't understand. Start off as you mean to continue!

You can practise lead training in the garden.

THE OUTSIDE WORLD

The next stage is introducing your puppy to the outside world – and, again, this should be done as soon as possible. While you are waiting for the puppy to finish his course of injections, it is really only safe to allow him to play in the garden and not venture out into public places. This will allow him to hear certain sounds, perhaps cars or lorries in the distance, but this is only a limited amount of socialisation. Once you have the all-clear from your vet, then do make every effort to take your puppy out into the big, wide world.

It is always a good idea to practise with the lead and collar in the garden (see Chapter 6). This way, when you do venture out on the pathways, your pup will walk alongside you, rather than steaming ahead on the lead or dragging behind. The first few walks are always the more exciting and interesting, as there are lots of new things for your pup to see and hear, so be patient – this is a whole new world to your Golden pup.

It is not uncommon for puppies to show some degree of fear at this stage, but you must react in a positive manner. Call his name and praise him verbally, but do not be tempted to pat him or cuddle him, as this runs the risk of reinforcing the fear and making the situation worse. Ignore the reaction and use play as a form of distraction.

Don't be tempted to over-exercise at this very early age, as you can damage the puppy's bones. Golden Retrievers are fast-growing and their bones are very soft for quite a while.

A good way of enabling your puppy or older dog to mix with other dogs is to attend socialisation classes. These are often run by vets, or, for older dogs, by local canine clubs. Golden Retrievers are very sociable dogs and adapt to this very well.

When taking on a rescued or older dog, then often the training required is more intense. If the dog needs help with any aspect of his behaviour, then enlist the help of a trainer or behaviourist. Many of these dogs have never been given much attention, so a one-to-one training session will help greatly.

VISITING THE VET

Before you collect your new puppy or older dog, register with a local vet, and take your new Golden Retriever for a health-check within a day or two of bringing him home. All my puppies leave us having had a complete health-check by my own vet – this is for my peace of mind and the new owner's. However, I always advise my new owners to take their new puppy to their own vet as soon as they can, so they can discuss inoculations and other details.

Another point to discuss with your vet is suitable identification. As a breeder, all my puppies leave me having been tattooed inside their ear; it is a quick and neat method, which gives each puppy an individual number, which is then registered on a national database.

Most vets use the microchip, which is inserted by a needle into the puppy's neck; it has a unique number, which can be matched to the owner's details when scanned.

It is important that your puppy enjoys his visit to the vet, to avoid him being fearful when older. Take some treats along, and ask the vet to give some to your dog, so your Golden Retriever learns that these vet visits are fun.

SUMMARY

A happy and contented dog is a great source of pleasure and the rewards of owning a Golden Retriever are numerous. By taking the time to understand your puppy's needs, from a physical and social perspective, you can help to ensure that he grows up to be a calm, obedient and social dog who is a pleasure to own and a welcome member of your community.

Enjoy your new puppy. They grow up very quickly, but a Golden Retriever is always a puppy at heart.

The art of rearing is to see the world from your puppy's perspective and to understand his needs.

THE BEST
OF CARE

Chapter 5

We are fortunate that the Golden Retriever is a relatively easy dog to care for, and providing you cater for his basic needs, he should live a long, happy and healthy life. A Golden Retriever needs a balanced diet, which consists of the same nutritional components that are required in our own diet. These include the following:

CARBOHYDRATES
Carbohydrates are needed as a source of energy for dogs, and some of the starchy complex carbohydrates are useful in maintaining regular gut movements. There are two types of carbohydrate: simple carbohydrates are the sugars, which can be found naturally in fruit and vegetables; refined carbohydrates are found in prepared food and sweets.

Carbohydrates are the 'sugars and starches' in the diet and are broken down in the dog's body to form glucose, which is transported around the body in blood. Carbohydrates are provided in the diet by biscuits, vegetables, rice and pulses.

FATS
Fats provide at least twice as much energy per gram as carbohydrates. This is important at times when an extra energy source is needed, such as in growing puppies or in pregnant and lactating bitches. Unsaturated fats contain 'fatty acids' and without these the coat may look dull, healing of wounds can be affected, and there may be reproductive problems. Vegetable sources or oily fish can provide fatty acids in the diet. Oily fish contains the Omega 3 fats, which are said to promote health and wellbeing.

Saturated fats are mostly solid at room temperature and are usually found in animal and dairy products. These are the fats that can be more harmful if consumed in excess.

PROTEIN
Protein is needed for growth, tissue maintenance and repair. Protein is made up of a number of amino acids, some of which cannot be made within the body. Meat, fish, dairy products and eggs contain all the essential amino acids needed by the body.

The protein derived from vegetables, pulses, cereals, legumes and vegetarian proteins, such as Quorn, contain many of the amino acids, but you need to combine a number of different plant proteins to make up the complete range of amino acids required by a dog.

An active, healthy dog needs a well-balanced diet.

VITAMINS AND MINERALS

Vitamins and minerals are needed in small quantities. They are added to complete and tinned foods, and are found in most components of natural feeding. Some minerals need to be balanced, as they work together; therefore, you need to be aware of over-supplementing your dog. Vitamins are needed in small amounts, and your dog should be able to take in all he needs through regular feeding.

WATER

Fresh water must always be available for your dog, especially when feeding complete dried foods that need water to assist with their passage through the gut. Some people prefer to soak complete foods prior to feeding

so that they do not swell in the stomach. This can be especially important for puppies, who have smaller stomachs and therefore have less room for the food to expand. Soaking food can also be a good way of encouraging dogs that eat too quickly to slow down.

CHANGING NEEDS

The needs of a Golden Retriever will change as he grows from puppyhood through to old age. Puppies need extra calories to produce energy and promote growth, and therefore they need foods that are higher in carbohydrates and fats. Puppies are usually fed up to four or five times a day when they are weaned, as their stomachs are unable to take large amounts of

food at each mealtime. This is reduced as the pups grow, and most puppies are fed three of four times a day when they move to their new homes.

As a puppy grows, his diet will need to be changed to reflect the needs of a young dog. This usually means the amount of protein will be decreased to reduce the calorie intake. As a dog gets older and is able to eat larger amounts of food, so the number of meals can be reduced. In adult life, a dog can cope with being fed once a day, although many people advocate a twice-daily routine as being best for the dog.

When a Golden Retriever reaches his twilight years, his energy requirements decrease and therefore he does not require as many calories. There are diets especially produced for the older dog that take this into account. An older dog may also benefit from being fed two or three smaller meals a day.

FEEDING METHODS

When you are feeding your Golden Retriever, not only do you have to provide a balanced diet, you also need to decide how you are going to feed it. You can stick to conventional daily mealtimes, or you can weigh up the pros and cons of free feeding or weekly fasting.

FREE FEEDING

This method is when a dog has constant free access to food. There are advocates for free feeding, but I would not

FOOD MANNERS

Whatever way you choose to feed your dog, you should always be able to remove the dish from him if you need to. This has the dual purpose of exerting your authority over the dog and ensuring he does not become possessive over food. This is extremely important, especially if there are children in the home who might inadvertently go near to the dog when he is eating. Food is a big issue with dogs, and no matter how loving your Golden is, his behaviour will change if he is allowed to 'guard' his food.

The best plan is train your dog to "Wait" when you put the bowl down, and to use a command such as "OK" when he can eat. In this way, the dog understands that you have control over his food and he may eat only when he is given permission. Most dogs learn this very quickly, and, as a result, all the stress is taken away from mealtimes for both dog and owner.

Teach your Golden Retriever to "Wait" when you put his food bowl down.

recommend it for a Golden Retriever for a number of reasons:

- The digestive system is never given time to rest.
- It is more difficult to house train youngsters, as there is no routine for feeding and excreting.
- It is very difficult to keep track of the quantity a dog is eating, and he could easily become overweight or underweight.
- If more than one dog is kept, it is difficult to ensure that each

individual is getting the correct amount.
- It negates the use of treats for training; a dog may not be as willing to work if food is always available.

FASTING

Some people advocate fasting a dog for one day, every week, to allow the gut to rest and to clear out the system. I have never tried this method as I use complete foods, which are developed to be fed every day. However, if you

prefer feeding in a more natural way, this would replicate the way in which a wild animal would feed. If you intend to do this, remember that water should always be available.

DIETARY CHOICES

There is a vast range of dietary choices on the market, which can be bewildering for the first-time dog owner. A breeder will rear a litter on the diet that most suits their own dogs, and you may well find that this is worth sticking

Complete diets are formulated to meet a dog's needs at different stages of his life.

Canned food is convenient to use – but check the nutritional balance.

Most dogs will relish a homemade diet, but you may need to add supplements.

with, at least to begin with. As noted earlier, it is important not to change the diet when a puppy is settling into his new home. However, if you have difficulty in getting hold of a particular diet, or your puppy is not thriving, you will need to examine the available options:

COMPLETE DIETS
Complete foods are the easiest and most convenient way of ensuring your dog gets the balanced diet he needs. These foods should not need supplementing, as all the requirements will be in the food.

In most cases, manufacturers of complete diets provide a range of foods that can be used from puppy through to senior. The amounts of protein, carbohydrate and fat will vary depending on which range of foods you use, as will the ingredients. There are special puppy formulas, which provide the optimum balance of proteins, carbohydrates and fats to cope with growth. There are junior, adult and senior varieties;

again, these provide the measured amounts of ingredients, which suit all the various stages of life. There is usually a guide to feeding on each pack but it pays to watch the weight of your dog and to change the amounts to suit the individual.

There are also diets that are gluten-free, or free from additives, which may be helpful if your puppy is allergic to some ingredients.

CANNED FOOD
A diet of canned meat or pouches with biscuit is easy to use and is readily available at pet shops or supermarkets. However, you will need to check the ingredients to be confident that your dog is getting all the nutrients he requires. In some cases, you may need to add vitamins and minerals.

HOME-MADE
In order to feed a home-made diet of fresh meat and biscuit, you will need to find a reliable

source of fresh or frozen meat and the facilities to store it. There are specialist companies that provide a range of frozen meat, and many pet stores offer frozen meats as part of their range. This diet may also need to be supplemented, as meat and biscuits on their own may not contain all of the vitamins and minerals needed to fulfil a dog's needs.

BARF DIET
The BARF diet is a holistic way of feeding your dog. BARF stands for Biologically Appropriate Raw Food, or Bones And Raw Food, and is based on feeding your dog raw meat and vegetables in order to reflect the way the ancestors of our dogs would have eaten in the wild. It also excludes cereals, grains and preservatives, which are seen by some as having a detrimental effect on the dog. A diet balanced with raw meat, fruit and vegetables should provide all of the vitamins and minerals that dogs need. Other benefits of feeding the BARF way include:

- Teeth are kept clean naturally and gum disease is prevented
- Strengthens jaw, neck and shoulder muscles, as these are used to rip at the raw meaty bones
- Produces smaller and firmer stools
- It is an economical diet.

The diet is based on feeding a balance of raw meat and liquidised fruit and vegetables on a 1:2 ratio. The fruit and vegetables are liquidised to make them more easily digestible. Raw bones should be fed once or twice a week, and raw offal once a week. There should be a variety of meats, fruit and vegetables to ensure your dog gets all the nutrients he needs.

If you change to a BARF diet, it is recommended that you do this gradually over a period of two weeks. There are lots of books and information available to help you if you choose this way of feeding.

FADDY FEEDERS

There may be good reasons why you decide to change your dog's diet, and, in all cases, this should be undertaken over a number of days, reducing the current food and replacing it gradually with the new food so that the dog is not affected by diarrhoea.

Golden Retrievers are generally enthusiastic about their food, but if your dog starts to get picky, do not keep changing the food to try to find something he likes. Constant change leads to stomach upsets, and it may affect

THE OLD-FASHIONED WAY

Breeders used to feed puppies on milk and cereals twice a day, and meat and biscuits twice a day, adding eggs and other treats for the growing dog. Nowadays, this is seen as being a bit hit-and-miss and too inconvenient for the average puppy owner.

The other drawback is that excessive cows' milk can upset a puppy's stomach because of the lactose content; goats' milk is much easier on the puppy's tummy, but it is not always readily available at a reasonable price.

Goldens love their food, so there is no need to introduce changes unless there is a good reason for it.

Keep a close eye on your Golden Retriever's weight – obesity is the cause of many health problems.

the growth and development of a puppy. It can also lead to a puppy becoming a faddy feeder, constantly refusing food to see what else you might offer. Before you know it, your dog will refuse to eat unless you have added tasty treats, such as chicken or fish, to his food.

Dogs do not seem to need a variety of different foods, as we humans do; therefore, when you have found the right type of food, stay with it unless your dog's needs change.

PROTEIN OVERLOAD
If your dog becomes over-excitable or unruly, it may be worth checking the levels of protein in his food and reducing the calorie intake. Protein overload can have a marked effect on a dog's behaviour.

Protein overload is a problem that often occurs when a dog is kept on a puppy formula food for a longer period than necessary, as this has a higher calorific value than junior or adult foods.

GOLDEN FATTIES
Golden Retrievers enjoy their food and they can easily become overweight. Care must be taken that the amount of food given is balanced with the exercise the dog receives and the amount of calories he needs. Extra calories are converted to fat and stored in the body. If your dog is overweight, you may notice that he is unable to walk more than short distances, and he may have difficulty in walking up slopes and steps. If you cannot feel your

dog's ribs and you cannot see a 'waist' (when looking from above), the chances are that your Golden is carrying too much weight.

If your dog is slightly overweight, reduce the quantity of food given, or reduce the protein content of the dog's food by using a 'lighter' version of the diet, remembering to change this over a number of days. If the dog is seriously obese, then seek advice from your veterinary surgeon, as there are special diet foods that can be prescribed.

TREATING YOUR DOG

There are many different types of treats available for dogs, and while these are invaluable as training aids and for keeping the dog's interest, the use of them must be taken into account when working out your dog's daily ration. If you have had a lengthy training session, using a lot of treats, you must reduce the quantity of food you give at mealtimes.

Some types of treat can be dangerous if given unsupervised. For example, care must be taken with pressed rawhide chews. A dog can chew off small pieces, which may then get stuck in the gut and cause digestive problems. Some of the highly coloured chews can affect the colour of the dog's excreta, and this may be

BONE OF CONTENTION

Do not give your Golden cooked chicken and lamb bones, as these can break, leaving very sharp edges that can damage the intestine. This could lead to serious problems and a large vet bill. The only safe bone to give is a smoked or a deep-fried marrowbone, removing any small pieces as the dog chews them.

disturbing for the owner.

There are dental chews, which help to keep the teeth free of tartar and keep gums healthy. These are fine to use as long as the dog is supervised.

USING ADDITIVES

Some people use additives to enhance their Golden Retriever's appearance and improve health. The use of garlic in the diet is said to repel fleas, and although there does not seem to be any research or documentary evidence that it works, it is generally found to be an effective deterrent.

Evening primrose oil is said to improve coat texture and appearance, and sunflower or olive oil helps older dogs who suffer with stiffness in their joints.

GROOMING GOLDENS

A Golden Retriever has the most beautiful coat, and this needs regular grooming and care to

keep it looking at its best. Your dog will need to be groomed every day; this not only is good for the dog, it also helps to build a good relationship between you. Most Goldens enjoy this time and will come running when they see you with a brush or comb in your hand.

A Golden Retriever should be brushed in the direction in which the hair grows. The best type of brush is one with flexible metal pins, which will move through the hair easily, without harming the dog's skin. You will need a metal comb for the featherings, which need to be gently combed through to remove tangles. The areas in which the hair can easily tangle are behind the ears, in the elbows, and in the groin area. If neglected, the hair can cause considerable discomfort to the dog.

Regular grooming with a good brush will also distribute the natural oils in the coat and give it a lovely sheen. If you want your Golden to look his stunning best, you can finish off by working over the coat with a hound glove. This has shorter metal pins on one side, which help to brush the hair into the correct place and add a glossy finish to the coat. The other side of the hound glove is made of material and can be used to 'buff up' the coat and really make it shine.

GROOMING

The Golden Retriever needs to be brushed in the direction that his coat lies. Start on the chest and work round to the neck.

Keep brushing along the length of the body.

The hindquarters will need thorough grooming, brushing through the layers of the coat.

Comb the fur behind the ears to prevent mats from forming.

Combing will also help to remove dead hair when your dog is shedding.

The feathering on the front legs needs attention.

Comb through the feathering on the undercarriage.

The tail has profuse feathering and needs daily combing.

Wipe the inside of the ears to keep them fresh and clean.

Teeth should be cleaned on a regular basis.

Use nail clippers to trim the tip of the nails.

Trim the hair that grows between the pads.

As well as brushing the coat, you need to check the general health of your dog. If you do this on a regular basis, you will detect any changes in your dog at an early stage. For example, if you find a lump, it can be checked and monitored by the vet. Grooming your dog also gives you the opportunity to check your dog's mouth, teeth and feet. By doing this regularly, the dog becomes used to being handled, and will willingly let the vet examine him if required.

EARS
Check your Golden's ears for discharge. Ears can be cleaned with drops that flush out any discharge, which can be wiped away with a clean wad of cotton wool. Any prolonged discharge or smell could indicate that veterinary attention may be required.

TEETH
Teeth need regular cleaning, using a special dog toothbrush and toothpaste; human toothpaste should not be used. Regularly chewing bones or chew toys specifically designed for oral health also help to keep teeth and gums healthy. A build-up of tartar on the teeth should be monitored; if necessary, ask the vet to clean the teeth while the dog is under anaesthetic. An accumulation of tartar can cause gum disease, and, as in humans, this can lead to more serious problems.

NAILS
A dog's nails should wear down naturally while road walking and therefore may not need any attention. However, some dogs have nails that continue to grow no matter how much road walking is done. If your Golden's nails grow too long, they will need to be clipped to a reasonable length either by yourself, if you have the confidence and know what you are doing, or by the vet. Care must be taken; if you cut into the quick, it will produce a copious amount of blood and may make your dog wary of having his nails clipped again.

TRIMMING
Goldens that are not shown do not need to be regularly trimmed, but it is important to keep the excess hair around the feet short, as longer hair will collect more mud to bring through your home. The tail may also become untidy and may need to be trimmed. In addition, to enhance the look of your dog, you can tidy up the excess hair around the ears and trouser featherings. You will need straight-edged scissors for trimming the feet and tail.

SHOW PRESENTATION

Show exhibitors trim their dogs to enhance outlines and hide faults. A judge will soon find these faults when he is doing a hands-on examination, and will recognise the tricks of the trade employed by trimming, but an exhibitor is entitled to present his dog to the best possible advantage.

- Trimming the hair at the front of the neck will make the neck look longer and more elegant. Thinning scissors are used for this, as they give a more subtle cut and the result therefore looks more natural.
- Tidying the tail feathering makes the dog look more balanced.
- Trimming around the feet gives a neater shape.

BATH-TIME

Golden Retrievers do not need to be regularly bathed unless they roll in something dreadful or swim in stagnant water. Bitches may need a bath after their season to remove any staining on the trouser featherings and to remove the 'in season bitch' smell so she is not bothered when she goes out in the vicinity of other dogs.

Bathing removes the natural oils from the coat and therefore can make it look fluffy until the oils are replaced and the coat gets back its natural sheen. There are many shampoos and conditioners especially formulated for dogs and some help with repelling insects, which can be a bonus.

If you do decide to bath your dog, you must ensure he is dried properly, especially around the tail. If a wet dog is left in the cold or in a draught, he can suffer from 'dead tail', which is a painful condition where the dog cannot hold his tail naturally and it looks limp or 'dead'. This will correct itself in a few days, but it does cause discomfort to the dog.

Use straight-edged scissors to trim the hair around the foot.

The trimmed foot (left) shows a marked contrast to the untrimmed foot.

PREVENTATIVE HEALTH CONTROLS

Worming should become part of your care routine; wormers purchased from your veterinary surgeon are usually more effective than those purchased over the counter. Generally, dogs are wormed at least twice a year, although some people advocate worming every three months. You will also need to check the coat for fleas and take preventative action on a regular basis with a spray or spot-on treatment. There are some 'spot on' flea preparations that also act as wormers, and these are used on a monthly basis. For more information on preventative health care, see Chapter 8.

SHOW PRESENTATION

Thinning scissors should be used on the neck (above) and chest (below) to enhance the Golden Retriever's contours.

Thin the hair behind the ears so that the ears lie flat.

The shape of the ears is enhanced by trimming with straight-edged scissors.

The tail is trimmed so the feathering falls into a graceful curve.

Groomed to perfection and ready for the show ring.

To begin with a puppy will get all the exercise he needs, playing in the garden.

EXERCISE

Golden Retriever puppies do not need a large amount of exercise in their first year, as this can affect their growth and have a detrimental effect upon their hip and elbow joints. A puppy will run around and play naturally, and then fall asleep when he is tired. However, formal exercise should be restricted. As a guide, a puppy should have approximately a minute of exercise for every week of his age. So, at 15 weeks, a pup could have 15 minutes of formal exercise; when he is a year old, he could cope with 52 minutes a day. This is only a guide, but it is useful for keeping exercise within reasonable limits.

As a dog moves into adulthood he is able to cope with longer periods of exercise, and a full-grown Golden Retriever will adjust to the exercise that is offered by his owners. Ideally, a walk should combine free-running and walking on a lead, which allows a dog to let off steam and then be under control, especially in busy areas.

If you walk your dog in a rural area, you need to be aware of farm animals and local wildlife, as there may be legal implications if your dog chases or kills livestock. Dogs should be kept on a lead near livestock, and it is also advisable to keep your dog on a lead if he is not reliable in obeying your commands. There may be local restrictions on some areas, such as beaches, at certain times of the year and you should make yourself aware of any local restrictions and abide by them. Most importantly, you should always clear up any mess made by your dog and dispose of it responsibly.

SWIMMING

Golden Retrievers love to swim. They like water – whether it is a large lake or a small puddle! They will seek out water and wade in

FIT AND HEALTHY

It is important to limit exercise while your Golden is still growing, to protect vulnerable bones and joints.

The fully-grown Golden Retriever will thrive on as much exercise as you can give him.

If you have more than one dog, they will use up a lot of energy playing together.

TAKING A DIP

There are few Goldens who can resist the chance of a swim – particularly when a retrieve is part of the game.

Stand back for the inevitable shake!

the smaller puddles or swim in the deeper water. Swimming is excellent exercise for dogs; there are hydrotherapy pools where you can take your dog for remedial exercise after injury or surgical interventions, or just for fitness and fun. I regularly take my dogs for swimming at a local hydrotherapy pool. They retrieve toys from the water for the whole session, and have to be almost dragged out when it's time to leave.

When your dog is swimming, it is best to remove his collar. There have been fatal accidents when a dog has caught his feet in his collar and drowned.

PLAYING GAMES

As Golden Retrievers have a great sense of smell, it is easy to train your dog to find hidden articles and bring them back to you. This is fun for the dog and it can be useful if you lose something, as you can call on

your dog's in-built talents to find it. A friend of mine lost her car keys in some grass and was able to get her Golden to seek them out.

Hiding from your dog when you are out walking will make him focus on you, and will encourage him not to stray too far away when off-lead.

There are many toys available that are designed to enhance a dog's natural abilities. Some toys can be filled or stuffed with

GOLDEN OLDIES

The Golden Retriever is a breed that is usually long-lived and can easily reach the age of 15 years. Obviously, an older dog will slow up, and will be reliant on his creature comforts. He will still want to go out for daily exercise, but he may be slower and unable to go as far as once he was able to.

As a Golden gets older, the texture of his coat may change, which means he will need extra grooming so that the coat does not become matted. Dietary requirements may also change, especially if the dog has problems with his teeth. If you are concerned about this, ask your vet for advice.

It is likely that sight and hearing may deteriorate in old age, and the caring owner needs to be aware of the veteran's changing needs.

As your Golden Retriever gets older, you will need to consider his changing needs.

In time, you will be able to look back and remember all the happy times you spent with your beloved Golden.

food, and the dog needs to work out how to manipulate the toy to get at the food. This can provide entertainment for the dog – and for the owner watching the dog trying to solve the problem. I had a cube for my dogs, which dropped out food as they rolled it over. They soon learned how to get the food and the cube would be sent around the garden at great speed until all the food had dropped out. There are also retrieve articles, some of which are designed to bounce at strange angles when thrown, to develop the dog's natural retrieving instinct.

SAYING GOODBYE

The difficulty for all of us is that when a dog's health fails, we may be faced with the decision of whether to treat the condition or not. Euthanasia is the alternative, and this is never an easy decision to make. The factors that need to be taken into account include:

- Does the dog still enjoy a good quality of life?
- Are you keeping the dog alive for his sake, or simply because you can't bear to make a final decision?
- If the dog is on medication, are their side effects that cause

extra problems or discomfort to the dog.

Measuring quality of life will depend on the individual viewpoint, but you will know your own dog after the years you have spent together and will recognise when the quality has gone out of his life. Your dog will have been a much-loved friend, and letting him go with dignity is the last act of kindness you can give him. Sometimes we have to balance the impact of surgery or long-term treatment against what benefits the dog will gain.

The Golden Retriever is one of

RAINBOW BRIDGE

Just this side of heaven is a place called Rainbow Bridge.

When an animal dies that has been especially close to someone here, that pet goes to Rainbow Bridge. There are meadows and hills for all of our special friends so they can run and play together. There is plenty of food, water and sunshine, and our friends are warm and comfortable.

All the animals who had been ill and old are restored to health and vigour; those who were hurt or maimed are made whole and strong again, just as we remember them in our dreams of days and times gone by.

The animals are happy and content, except for one small thing: they each miss someone very special to them, who had to be left behind.

They all run and play together, but the day comes when one suddenly stops and looks into the distance. His bright eyes are intent; his eager body quivers. Suddenly he begins to run from the group, flying over the green grass, his legs carrying him faster and faster.

You have been spotted, and when you and your special friend finally meet, you cling together in joyous reunion, never to be parted again. The happy kisses rain upon your face; your hands again caress the beloved head, and you look once more into the trusting eyes of your pet, so long gone from your life but never absent from your heart.

Then you cross the Rainbow Bridge together...

the most expressive of dogs, and your Golden will look at you with his beautiful brown eyes and let you know he has had enough. Keeping your old friend alive just because you are unable to bear the loss is not fair and does a disservice to the dog. It is always better to make a decision one week early than one day too late.

Your vet will guide you through this process and give you the benefit of their professional opinion. If your dog finds visiting the surgery stressful, it may be kinder to ask the vet to visit you at home. Some people like to bury their

pets at home; others choose to have them cremated and keep the ashes in a casket or scatter them in a special place. My dogs' ashes are all scattered beneath the magnolia tree in my garden.

Some people find the death of a much-loved pet is as difficult as losing any other member of the family, and their grief can be just as acute. In some cases, the best way forward is to get another dog, but others cannot bear the thought of 'finding a replacement'. It is sometimes difficult for friends or family who are not dog lovers to recognise how the loss of a pet impacts on individuals, but there is help out

there from pet bereavement counsellors. The internet is another useful resource, where you can gain support from other people who have lost a much-loved pet.

You may also need to take into account how other animals in the family can be affected by the loss, especially those who have always lived together, and time should be taken to help them come to terms with the loss.

The loss of your dog will be difficult, but you need to remember the good times you had together and that the decision you made was in the best interest of your dog.

TRAINING AND SOCIALISATION

Chapter 6

When you decided to bring a Golden Retriever into your life, you probably had dreams of how it was going to be: long walks together, cosy evenings with a Golden lying devotedly at your feet, and a special welcome waiting for you whenever you returned home.

There is no doubt that you can achieve all this – and much more – with a Golden, but like anything that is worth having, you must be prepared to put in the work. A Golden, regardless of whether it is a puppy or an adult, does not come ready trained, understanding exactly what you want and fitting perfectly into your lifestyle. A Golden has to learn his place in your family and he must discover what is acceptable behaviour.

We have a great starting point in that the Golden has an outstanding temperament. The breed was developed to be a biddable shooting companion, and all Goldens are kind, friendly and eager to please. The Golden is also an intelligent dog, so we have all the ingredients needed to produce a well-trained, well-behaved companion.

THE FAMILY PACK

Dogs have been domesticated for some 14,000 years, but, luckily for us, they have inherited and retained behaviour from their distant ancestor – the wolf. A Golden Retriever may never have lived in the wild, but he is born with the survival skills and the mentality of a meat-eating predator who hunts in a pack. A wolf living in a pack owes its existence to mutual co-operation and an acceptance of a hierarchy, as this ensures both food and protection. A domesticated dog

living in a family pack has exactly the same outlook. He wants food, companionship and leadership – and it is your job to provide for these needs.

YOUR ROLE

Theories about dog behaviour and methods of training go in and out of fashion, but in reality, nothing has changed from the day when wolves ventured in from the wild to join the family circle. The wolf (and equally the dog) accepts a subservient place in the family pack in return for food and protection. In a dog's eyes, you are his leader, and he relies on you to make all the important decisions. This does not mean that you have to act like a dictator or a bully. You are accepted as a leader, without argument, as long as you have the right credentials.

The first part of the job is easy. You are the provider, and you are

Can you be a firm, fair and consistent leader?

There are a number of guidelines
to follow to establish yourself in
the role of leader in a way that
your Golden understands and
respects. If you have a puppy,
you may think you don't have to
take this on board for a few
months, but that would be a big
mistake. Start as you mean to go
on, and your pup will be quick to
find his place in his new family.

- **Keep it simple:** Decide on the
  rules you want your Golden to
  obey and always make it 100
  per cent clear what is
  acceptable, and what is
  unacceptable, behaviour.
- **Be consistent:** If you are not
  consistent about enforcing
  rules, how can you expect your
  Golden to take you seriously?
  There is nothing worse than
  allowing your Golden to jump
  up at you one moment and
  then scolding him the next
  time he does it because you are
  wearing your best clothes. As
  far as the Golden is concerned,
  he may as well try it on
  because he can't predict your
  reaction.
- **Get your timing right:** If you
  are rewarding your Golden, and
  equally if you are reprimanding
  him, you must respond within
  one to two seconds otherwise
  the dog will not link his
  behaviour with your reaction
  (see page 91).
- **Read your dog's body
  language:** Find out how to
  read body language and facial
  expressions (see page 90) so
  that you understand your

therefore respected because you
supply food. In a Golden's eyes,
you must be the ultimate hunter
because a day never goes by
when you cannot find food. The
second part of the leader's job
description is straightforward, but
for some reason we find it hard
to achieve. In order for a dog to
accept his place in the family

pack he must respect his leader
as the decision-maker. A low-
ranking pack animal does not
question authority; he is perfectly
happy to see someone else
shoulder the responsibility.
Problems will only arise if you cut
a poor figure as leader and the
dog feels he should mount a
challenge for the top-ranking role.

If you are expressive in your body language, your Golden Retriever will understand what you want him to do.

Golden's feelings and his intentions.

- **Be aware of your own body language:** When you ask your Golden to do something, do not bend over him and talk to him at eye level. Assert your authority by standing over him and keeping an upright posture. Obviously if you have a timid dog, you would not seek to make him more fearful by doing this. You can also help your dog to learn by using your body language to communicate with him. For example, if you want your dog to come to you, open your arms out and look inviting. If you want your dog to stay, use a hand signal (palm flat, facing the dog) so you are effectively 'blocking' his advance.
- **Tone of voice:** Dogs are very receptive to tone of voice, so

you can use your voice to praise him or to correct undesirable behaviour. If you are pleased with your Golden, praise him to the skies in a warm, happy voice. If you want to stop him raiding the bin, use a deep, stern voice when you say "No".

- **Give one command only:** If you keep repeating a command, or keeping changing it, your Golden will think you are babbling and will probably ignore you. If your Golden does not respond the first time you ask, make it simple by using a treat to lure him into position, and then you can reward him for a correct response.
- **Daily reminders:** A young, exuberant Golden Retriever is apt to forget his manners from time to time, and an adolescent dog may attempt to challenge

your authority (see page 107). Rather than coming down on your Golden like a ton of bricks when he does something wrong, try to prevent bad manners by daily reminders of good manners. For example:
  i Do not let your dog barge ahead of you when you are going through a door.
  ii Do not let him leap out of the car the moment you open the door (which could be potentially lethal, as well as being disrespectful).
  iii Do not let him eat from your hand when you are at the table.
  iv Do not let him 'win' a toy at the end of a play session and then make off with it. You 'own' his toys, and you must end every play session on your terms.

If you learn to read your Golden's body language you will understand his intentions. This dog is fascinated by the kitten, but he is showing that he is no threat, and will not chase.

UNDERSTANDING YOUR GOLDEN

Body language is an important means of communication between dogs, which they use to make friends, to assert status, and to avoid conflict. It is important to get on your dog's wavelength by understanding his body language and reading his facial expressions.

- A positive body posture and a wagging tail indicate a happy, confident dog.

- A crouched body posture with ears back and tail down show that a dog is being submissive. A dog may do this when he is being told off or if a more assertive dog approaches him.
- A bold dog will stand tall, looking strong and alert. His ears will be forward and his tail will be held high.
- A dog who raises his hackles (lifting the fur along his topline) is trying to look as scary as possible. This may be the prelude to aggressive

behaviour, but, in many cases, the dog is apprehensive and is unsure how to cope with a situation.
- A playful dog will go down on his front legs while standing on his hind legs in a bow position. This friendly invitation says: "I'm no threat; let's play."
- A dominant, aggressive dog will meet other dogs with a hard stare. If he is challenged, he may bare his teeth and growl, and the corners of his mouth will be drawn forward. His ears

will be forward and he will appear tense in every muscle.

- A nervous dog will often show aggressive behaviour as a means of self-protection. If threatened, this dog will lower his head and flatten his ears. The corners of his mouth may be drawn back, and he may bark or whine.
- A Golden believes in giving a big greeting. He will come up, tail wagging, with the inevitable 'gift' of a sock or a toy – or anything else he can find. Some Goldens will also 'talk' to you, making a deep, rumbling sound at the back of their throat. Do not mistake this for grumbling; it is a Golden's way of saying hello.

GIVING REWARDS

Why should your Golden do as you ask? If you follow the guidelines given above, your Golden should respect your authority, but what about the time when he is playing with a new doggy friend or has found a really enticing scent? The answer is that you must always be the most interesting, the most attractive, and the most irresistible person in your Golden's eyes. It would be nice to think you could achieve this by personality alone, but most of us need a little extra help. You need to find out what is the biggest reward for your dog. Most Golden Retrievers are food-orientated, but some have a favourite toy and their reward will be a play session with the toy.

When you are teaching a dog a new exercise, you should reward him frequently. When he knows the exercise or command, reward him randomly so that he keeps on responding to you in a positive manner. If your dog does something extra special, like leaving his canine chum mid-play in the park, make sure he really knows how pleased you are by giving him a handful of treats or throwing his ball a few extra times. If he gets a bonanza reward, he is more likely to come back on future occasions, because you have proved to be even more rewarding than his previous activity.

TOP TREATS
Some trainers grade treats depending on what they are asking the dog to do. A dog may get a low-grade treat, such as a piece of dry food, to reward good behaviour on a random basis, such as sitting when you open a door or allowing you to examine his teeth. But high-grade treats, which may be cooked liver, sausage or cheese, are reserved for training new exercises or for use in the park when you want a really good recall. Golden Retrievers are clever dogs, and you may well find that your dog gives that little bit extra if you have something that is worth working for. Whatever type of treat you use, remember to subtract it from your Golden's daily ration. Fat Goldens are lethargic, prone to health problems, and will almost certainly have a shorter life expectancy. Reward your Golden, but always keep a check on his figure!

HOW DO DOGS LEARN?
It is not difficult to get inside your Golden's head and understand how he learns, as it is not dissimilar to the way we learn. Dogs learn by conditioning: they find out that specific behaviours produce

THE CLICKER REVOLUTION

Karen Pryor pioneered the technique of clicker training when she was working with dolphins. It is very much a continuation of Pavlov's work (see page 93) and makes full use of association learning.

Karen wanted to mark 'correct' behaviour at the precise moment it happened. She found it was impossible to toss a fish to a dolphin when it was in mid-air, when she wanted to reward it. Her aim was to establish a conditioned response so the dolphin knew that it had performed correctly and a reward would follow.

The solution was the clicker: a small matchbox-shaped training aid, with a metal tongue that makes a click when it is pressed. To begin with, the dolphin had to learn that a click meant that food was coming. The dolphin then learnt that it

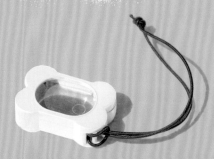

must 'earn' a click in order to get a reward. Clicker training has been used with many different animals, most particularly with dogs, and it has proved hugely successful. It is a great aid for pet owners and is also widely used by professional trainers who teach highly specialised skills.

specific consequences. This is known as operant conditioning or consequence learning. Consequences have to be immediate or clearly linked to the behaviour, as a dog sees the world in terms of action and result. Dogs will quickly learn if an action has a bad consequence or a good consequence.

Dogs also learn by association. This is known as classical conditioning or association learning. It is the type of learning made famous by Pavlov's experiment with dogs. Pavlov presented dogs with food and measured their salivary response (how much they drooled). Then he rang a bell just before presenting the food. At first, the dogs did not salivate until the food was presented. But after a while they learnt that the sound of the bell meant that food was coming, and so they salivated when they heard the bell. A dog needs to learn the association in order for it to have any meaning. For example, a dog that has never seen a lead before will be completely indifferent to

Try to find a training area that is free from distractions.

it. A dog that has learnt that a lead means he is going for a walk will get excited the second he sees the lead; he has learnt to associate a lead with a walk.

BE POSITIVE

The most effective method of training dogs is to use their ability to learn by consequence and to teach that the behaviour you want produces a good consequence. For example, if you ask your Golden to "Sit", and reward him with a treat, he will learn that it is worth his while to sit on command because it will lead to a treat. He is far more

likely to repeat the behaviour, and the behaviour will become stronger, because it results in a positive outcome. This method of training is known as positive reinforcement, and it generally leads to a happy, co-operative dog that is willing to work, and a handler who has fun training their dog.

The opposite approach is negative reinforcement. This is far less effective and often results in a poor relationship between dog and owner. In this method of training, you ask your Golden to "Sit", and, if he does not respond, you deliver a sharp yank on the training collar or push his rear to the ground. The dog learns that not responding to your command has a bad consequence, and he may be less likely to ignore you in the future. However, it may well have a bad consequence for you, too. A dog that is treated in this way may associate harsh handling with the handler and become aggressive or fearful. Instead of establishing a pattern of willing co-operation, you are establishing a relationship built on coercion.

GETTING STARTED

As you train your Golden, you will develop your own techniques as you get to know what motivates him. You may decide to get involved with clicker training or you may prefer to go for a simple command-and-reward formula. It does not matter what form of training you use, as long as it is based on positive, reward-based methods.

There are a few important guidelines to bear in mind when you are training your Golden:

- Find a training area that is free from distractions, particularly when you are just starting out.
- Keep training sessions short, especially with young puppies that have very short attention spans.
- Do not train if you are in a bad mood or if you are on a tight schedule – the training session will be doomed to failure.
- If you are using a toy as a reward, make sure it is only available when you are training. In this way it has an added value for your Golden.

- If you are using food treats, make sure they are bite-size and easy to swallow; you don't want to hang about while your Golden chews on his treat.
- All food treats must be deducted from your Golden's daily food ration.
- When you are training, move around your allocated area so that your dog does not think that an exercise can only be performed in one place.
- If your Golden is finding an exercise difficult, try not to get frustrated. Go back a step and praise him for his effort. You will probably find he is more successful when you try again at the next training session.
- Goldens are famous for having a stubborn streak, and it is not unusual for a puppy to dig his heels in and refuse to co-operate. If this happens, try coaxing with a treat. However, if your Golden still resists, give him a simple exercise to do so you can reward him. There is no point in pushing a Golden, or, worse still, using force. In most cases, a Golden will be ready to co-operate the next time you ask – as long as you have avoided a big confronation.
- Always end training sessions on a happy, positive note. Ask your Golden to do something you know he can do – it could be a trick he enjoys performing – and then reward him with a few treats or an extra-long play session.

In the exercises that follow, clicker training is introduced and

It will not take long before your Golden Retriever realises that he has to 'earn' a click in order to get a reward.

followed, but all the exercises will work without the use of a clicker.

INTRODUCING A CLICKER

This is an easy exercise, and a Golden, who is very quick to learn, will pick it up in no time. Initial clicker training can be combined with attention training, which is a very useful tool and can be used on many different occasions.

- Prepare some treats and go to an area that is free from distractions. When your Golden stops sniffing around and looks at you, click and reward by throwing him a treat. This means he will not crowd you, but will go looking for the treat. Repeat a couple of times. If your Golden is very easily distracted, you may need to start this exercise with the dog on a lead.
- After a few clicks, your Golden understands that if he hears a click, he will get a treat. He must now learn that he must 'earn' a click. This time, when your Golden looks at you, wait a little longer before clicking, and then reward him. If your Golden is on a lead but responding well, try him off the lead.
- When your Golden is working for a click and giving you his attention, you can introduce a cue or command word, such as "Watch". Repeat a few times, using the cue. You now have a Golden that understands the clicker and will give you his attention when you ask him to "Watch".

TRAINING EXERCISES

THE SIT

This is the easiest exercise to teach, so it is rewarding for both you and your Golden.

- Choose a tasty treat and hold it just above your puppy's nose. As he looks up at the treat, he will naturally go into the Sit. As soon as he is in position, reward him.
- Repeat the exercise, and when your pup understands what you want, introduce the "Sit" command.
- You can practise at mealtimes by holding out the bowl and waiting for your dog to sit. Most Goldens learn this one very quickly!

Start by luring your dog into the Sit.

Lower the treat to the ground, and your Golden will follow it, going into the Down position.

Work on getting an enthusiastic response for recalls.

THE DOWN

Work hard at this exercise, as a reliable Down is useful in many different situations, and an instant Down can be a lifesaver.

- You can start with your dog in a Sit, or it is just as effective to teach it when the dog is standing. Hold a treat just below your puppy's nose, and slowly lower it towards the ground. The treat acts as a lure, and your puppy will follow it, first going down on his forequarters and then bringing his hindquarters down as he tries to get the treat.
- Make sure you close your fist around the treat, and only reward your puppy with the treat when he is in the correct position. If your puppy is reluctant to go Down, you can apply gentle pressure on his shoulders to encourage him to go into the correct position.
- When your puppy is following the treat and going into position, introduce a verbal command.
- Build up this exercise over a period of time, each time waiting a little longer before giving the reward, so the puppy learns to stay in the Down position.

THE RECALL

It is never too soon to start training the Recall. In fact, if you have a puppy, it is best to start almost from the moment the puppy arrives home, as he has a strong instinct to follow you. Make sure you are always happy and excited when your Golden comes to you, even if he has been slower than you would like. Your Golden must believe that the greatest reward is coming to you.

- You can start teaching the Recall from the moment your puppy arrives home. He will naturally follow you, so keep calling his name and rewarding him when he comes to you.
- Practise in the garden, and when your puppy is busy exploring, get his attention by calling his name, and as he runs towards you, introduce the verbal command "Come". Make sure you sound happy

SECRET WEAPON

You can build up a strong Recall by using another form of association learning. Buy a whistle and peep on it when you are giving your Golden his food. You can choose the type of signal you want to give: two short peeps or one long whistle, for example. Within a matter of days, your dog will learn that the sound of the whistle means that food is coming.

Now transfer the lesson outside. Arm yourself with some tasty treats and the whistle. Allow your Golden to run free in the garden, and, after a couple of minutes, use the whistle. The dog has already learnt to associate the whistle with food, so he will come towards you. Immediately reward him with a treat

and lots of praise. Repeat the lesson a few times in the garden so you are confident that your dog is responding before trying it in the park. Make sure you always have some treats in your pocket when you go for a walk, and your dog will quickly learn how rewarding it is to come to you.

and exciting, so your puppy wants to come to you. When he responds, give him lots of praise.
- If your puppy is slow to respond, try running away a few paces, or jumping up and down. It doesn't matter how silly you look; the key issue is to get your puppy's attention, and then make yourself irresistible!
- In a dog's mind, coming when called should be regarded as the best fun because he knows he is always going to be rewarded. Never make the mistake of telling your dog off, no matter how slow he is to respond, as you will undo all your previous hard work.
- When you are free-running

your dog, make sure you have his favourite toy or a pocket full of treats so you can reward him at intervals throughout the walk when you call him to you.
- Do not allow your dog to run free and only call him back at the end of the walk to clip on his lead. An intelligent Golden will soon realise that the Recall means the end of his walk and then the end of fun – so who can blame him for not wanting to come back?

TRAINING LINE

This is the equivalent of a very long lead, which you can buy at a pet store, or you can make your own with a length of rope. The training line is attached to your Golden's collar and should be

around 15 feet (4.5 metres) in length.

The purpose of the training line is to prevent your Golden from disobeying you so that he never has the chance to get into bad habits. For example, when you call your Golden and he ignores you, you can immediately pick up the end of the training line and call him again. By picking up the line, you will have attracted his attention, and if you call in an excited, happy voice, your Golden will come to you. The moment he comes to you, give him a tasty treat so he is instantly rewarded for making the 'right' decision.

The training line is very useful when your Golden becomes an adolescent and is testing your leadership. When you have reinforced the correct behaviour a number of times, your dog will build up a strong recall and you will not need to use a training line.

WALKING ON A LOOSE LEAD

This is a simple exercise, which baffles many Golden owners. In most cases, owners are too impatient, wanting to get on with the expedition rather that

training the dog how to walk on a lead. Take time with this one; the Golden – particularly a male – is a strong dog, and a Golden that pulls on the lead is no pleasure to own.

With practice, your Golden will learn to walk on a loose lead.

- In the early stages of lead training, allow your puppy to pick his route and follow him. He will get used to the feeling of being 'attached' to you, and has no reason to put up any resistance.
- Next, find a toy or a treat and show it to your puppy. Let him follow the treat/toy for a few paces, and then reward him. Some Goldens can be stubborn when it comes to lead walking. If you are having problems, find a really tasty treat, such as a piece of cheese, and coax your puppy to take a few steps. Be lavish in your praise when the puppy co-operates; remember that he does like to please you. Never lose your temper or yank the lead, or you will make the situation worse.
- Build up the amount of time your pup will walk with you, and when he is walking nicely by your side, introduce the verbal command "Heel" or "Close". Give lots of praise when your pup is in the correct position.
- When your Golden puppy is walking alongside you, keep focusing his attention on you by using his name, and then reward him when he looks at you. If it is going well, introduce some changes of direction.

Build up the Stay exercise in easy stages. As your dog gets more experienced, you can circle round him before returning to his side.

- Do not attempt to take your puppy out on the lead until you have mastered the basics at home. You need to be confident that your puppy accepts the lead and will focus his attention on you, when requested, before you face the challenge of a busy environment.

- As your Golden gets bigger and stronger, he may try to pull on the lead, particularly if you are heading somewhere he wants to go, such as the park. If this happens, stop, call your dog to you, and do not set off again until he is in the correct position. It may take time, but your Golden will eventually realise that it is more productive to walk by your side than to pull ahead.

STAYS

This may not be the most exciting exercise, but it is one of the most useful. There are many occasions when you want your Golden to stay in position, even if it is only for a few seconds. The classic example is when you want your Golden to stay in the back of the car until you have clipped on his lead. Some trainers use the verbal command "Stay" when the dog is to remain in position for an extended period of time, and "Wait" if the dog is to stay in position for a few seconds until you give the next command. Others trainers use a universal "Stay" to cover all situations. It's down to personal preference, and as long as you are consistent, your dog will

understand the command given.

Put your puppy in a Sit or a Down, and use a hand signal (flat palm, facing the dog) to show he is to stay in position. Step a pace away from the dog. Wait a second, step back and reward him. If you have a lively pup, you may find it easier to train this exercise on the lead.

Repeat the exercise, gradually increasing the distance you can leave your dog. When you return to your dog's side, praise him quietly, and release him with a command, such as "Okay". Remember to keep your body language very still when you are training this exercise, and avoid eye contact with your dog. Work on this exercise over a period of time, and you will build up a really reliable Stay.

SOCIALISATION

While your Golden is mastering basic obedience exercises, there is other, equally important, work to do with him. A Golden is not only becoming a part of your home and family, he is becoming a member of the community. He needs to be able to live in the outside world, coping calmly with every new situation that comes his way. It is your job to introduce him to as many different experiences as possible and to encourage him to behave in an appropriate manner.

In order to socialise your Golden effectively, it is helpful to understand how his brain is developing, and then you will get a perspective on how he sees the world.

A young Golden Retriever will soak up new experiences like a sponge.

CANINE SOCIALISATION (Birth to 7 weeks)

This is the time when a dog learns how to be a dog. By interacting with his mother and his littermates, a young pup learns about leadership and submission. He learns to read body posture so that he understands the intentions of his mother and his siblings. A puppy that is taken away from his litter too early may always have behavioural problems with other dogs, either being fearful or aggressive.

SOCIALISATION PERIOD (7 to 12 weeks)

This is the time to get cracking and introduce your Golden puppy to as many different experiences as possible. This includes meeting different people, other dogs and animals, seeing new sights, and hearing a range of sounds, from the vacuum cleaner to the roar of traffic. At this stage, a puppy learns very quickly and what he learns will stay with him for the rest of his life. This is the best time for a puppy to move to a new home, as he is adaptable and ready to form deep bonds.

FEAR-IMPRINT PERIOD (8 to 11 weeks)

This occurs during the socialisation period, and it can be the cause of problems if it is not handled carefully. If a pup is exposed to a frightening or painful experience, it will lead to lasting impressions. Obviously, you will attempt to avoid

Supervise all interactions so that you can reward the behaviour you want.

frightening situations, such as your pup being bullied by a mean-spirited older dog, or a firework going off, but you cannot always protect your puppy from the unexpected. If your pup has a nasty experience, the best plan is to make light of it and distract him by offering him a treat or a game. The pup will take the lead from you and will be reassured that there is nothing to worry about. If you mollycoddle him and sympathise with him, he is far more likely to retain the memory of his fear.

SENIORITY PERIOD (12 to 16 weeks)

During this period, your Golden puppy starts to cut the apron strings and becomes more independent. He will test out his status to find out who is the pack leader: him or you. Bad habits, such as play biting, which may have been seen as endearing a

few weeks earlier, should be firmly discouraged. Remember to use positive, reward-based training, but make sure your puppy knows that you are the leader and must be respected.

SECOND FEAR-IMPRINT PERIOD (6 to 14 months)

This period is not as critical as the first fear-imprint period, but it should still be handled carefully. During this time your Golden may appear apprehensive or he may show fear of something familiar. A typical Golden reaction is to 'spook', and then try to run away from whatever is frightening him. Your job is to remain completely calm and to behave in a no-nonsense fashion. Use a treat to get your Golden's attention, and then give him lots of praise. Do not make your dog confront the thing that frightens him. Simply get his attention and give him something else to think

about, such as obeying a simple command, such as "Sit" or "Down". This will give you the opportunity to praise and reward your dog, and will help to boost his confidence.

A big mistake with Golden owners is being too 'nice' in this situation. Obviously, you sympathise with your dog's fear, but if you show too much concern, he will start thinking that there really is something to worry about. A clever Golden may also start playing you up, to get attention. The best advice is to be firm, yet kind.

YOUNG ADULTHOOD AND MATURITY (1 to 4 years)

The timing of this phase depends on the size of the dog: the bigger the dog, the later it is. This period coincides with a dog's increased size and strength, mental as well as physical. Some dogs, particularly those with a

101

dominant nature, will test your leadership again and may become aggressive towards other dogs. Firmness and continued training are essential at this time so that your Golden accepts his status in the family pack.

IDEAS FOR SOCIALISATION
When you are socialising your Golden, you want him to experience as many different situations as possible. But it is important to bear in mind that Golden Retrievers have long

memories; if a Golden has a negative experience, it may shape his behaviour for life. Plan where you are going to take your Golden Retriever, and work at building his confidence so he feels he can cope with anything, or anyone, he comes across. A mature, well-socialised Golden Retriever will be calm and laidback in all situations.

If you are taking on a rescued dog and have little knowledge of his background, it is important to work through a programme of socialisation. A young puppy soaks up new experiences like a sponge, but an older dog can still learn. If a rescued dog shows fear or apprehension, treat him in exactly the same way as you would treat a youngster who is going through the second fear-imprint period (see page 101).

- Accustom your puppy to household noises, such as the vacuum cleaner, the television and the washing machine.
- Ask visitors to come to the door, wearing different types of clothing – for example, wearing a hat or a long raincoat, or carrying a stick or an umbrella.
- If you do not have children at home, make sure your Golden has a chance to meet and play with them. Go to a local park and watch children in the play area. You will not be able to take your Golden inside the play area, but he will see children playing and will get used to their shouts of excitement.

The aim is to have a well-adjusted dog who will take all new situations in his stride.

TRAINING CLUBS

There are lots of training clubs to choose from. Your vet will probably have details of clubs in your area, or you can ask friends who have dogs if they attend a club. Alternatively, use the internet to find out more information. But how do you know if the club is any good?

Before you take your dog, ask if you can go to a class as an observer and find out the following:

- What experience does the instructor(s) have?
- Do they have experience with Golden Retrievers?
- Is the class well organised, and are the dogs reasonably quiet? (A noisy class indicates an unruly atmosphere, which will not be conducive to learning).
- Are there are a number of classes to suit dogs of different ages and abilities?
- Are positive, reward-based training methods used?
- Does the club train for the Good Citizen Scheme (see page 113)?

If you are not happy with the training club, find another one. An inexperienced instructor who cannot handle a number of dogs in a confined environment can do more harm than good.

- Attend puppy classes. These are designed for puppies between the ages of 12 to 20 weeks, and give puppies a chance to play and interact together in a controlled, supervised environment. Your vet will have details of a local class.
- Take a walk around some quiet streets, such as a residential area, so your Golden can get used to the sound of traffic. As he becomes more confident, progress to busier areas. Some Golden Retrievers are sensitive to sound, and the noise of a car or a lorry coming up from behind may be a source of concern. If your Golden is wary of traffic, find a bench where you can sit with your dog and spend some time letting him get used to the situation. Bring some treats along and reward him every now and again, so that he is distracted from the traffic and builds up a good association with being out in a busy environment.
- Go to a railway station. You don't have to get on a train if you don't need to, but your Golden will have the chance to experience trains, people wheeling luggage, loudspeaker announcements, and going up and down stairs and over railway bridges.
- If you live in the town, plan a trip to the country. You can enjoy a day out and provide an opportunity for your Golden to see livestock, such as sheep, cattle and horses.
- One of the best places for socialising a dog is at a country fair. There will be crowds of people, livestock in pens, tractors, bouncy castles, fairground rides and food stalls.
- When your dog is over 20 weeks of age, find a training class for adult dogs. You may find that your local training class has both puppy and adult classes.

THE ADOLESCENT GOLDEN

It happens to every dog – and every owner. One minute you have an obedient well-behaved youngster, and the next you have a boisterous adolescent who appears to have forgotten everything he learnt. This applies equally to males and females, although the type of adolescent behaviour, and its onset, varies between individuals.

In most cases a Golden male will hit adolescence between 12 to 18 months. This is a slow-maturing breed, and you may have to wait until your Golden is two years old before he is fully mature. In most cases, a male Golden will be harder to train at this time. Although the breed is very biddable, a male Golden has a mind of his own, and during adolescence he will test the boundaries. A dog who had a perfect recall may well become distracted, picking up an airborne scent, or putting his nose to the ground and ignoring your calls.

Female Goldens show adolescent behaviour as they approach their first season, which could be as early as six months of age. At this time, a female Golden may become a little moody and withdrawn. She may prefer to be left on her own rather than

Despite your best efforts, there may be a time when you encounter behavioural problems.

enjoying interaction with her human family. However, as soon as her hormones have settled down, she will return to being her usual loving self.

In reality, adolescence is not the nightmare period you may imagine, if you see it from your Golden's perspective. With females Goldens, it is best to respect their feelings and not fuss them too much at this trying period. With a male Golden, who is attempting to flex his muscles and challenge your role as leader, you must be firm, fair and consistent. If you show that you are a strong leader (see pag 88) and are quick to reward good

behaviour, your Golden will accept you as his protector and provider.

WHEN THINGS GO WRONG

Positive, reward-based training has proved to be the most effective method of teaching dogs, but what happens when your Golden does something wrong and you need to show him that his behaviour is unacceptable? The old-fashioned school of dog training used to rely on the powers of punishment and negative reinforcement. A dog who raided the bin, for example, was smacked. Now we have learnt that it is not only unpleasant and cruel to hit a dog, it is also ineffective. If you hit a dog for stealing, he is more than likely to see you as the bad consequence of stealing, so he may raid the bin again, but probably not when you are around. If he raided the bin some time before you discovered it, he will be even more confused by your punishment, as he will not relate your response to his 'crime'.

A more commonplace example is when a dog fails to respond to a recall in the park. When the dog eventually comes back, the owner puts the dogs on the lead and goes straight home to punish the dog for his poor response.

Unfortunately, the dog will have a different interpretation. He does not think: "I won't ignore a recall command because the bad consequence is the end of my play in the park." He thinks: "Coming to my owner resulted in the end of playtime – therefore coming to my owner has a bad consequence, so I won't do that again."

There are a number of strategies to tackle undesirable behaviour – and they have nothing to do with harsh handling.

Ignoring bad behaviour: A lot of undesirable behaviour in young Goldens is to do with over-exuberance. This trait is part of the breed's charm, but it can lead to difficult and sometimes dangerous situations. For example, a young Golden that repeatedly jumps up at visitors will eventually knock someone over unless he is stopped. In this case, the Golden is seeking attention, and so the best plan is to ignore him. Do not look at him, do not speak to him, and do not push him down – all these actions are rewarding for your Golden. But someone who turns their back on him and offers no response is plain boring. The moment your Golden has four feet on the ground, give him lots of praise and maybe a treat. If you repeat this often enough, the Golden will learn that jumping up does not have any good consequences, such as getting attention. Instead he is ignored. However, when he has

all four feet on the ground, he gets loads of attention. He links the action with the consequence, and chooses the action that is most rewarding. You will find that this strategy works well with all attention-seeking behaviour, such as barking, whining or scrabbling at doors. Being ignored is a worst-case scenario for a Golden, so remember to use it as an effective training tool.

Stopping bad behaviour: There are occasions when you want to

call an instant halt to whatever it is your Golden is doing. He may have just jumped on the sofa, or you may have caught him red-handed in the rubbish bin. He has already committed the 'crime', so your aim is to stop him and to redirect his attention. You can do this by using a deep, firm tone of voice to say "No", which will startle him, and then call him to you in a bright, happy voice. If necessary, you can attract him with a toy or a treat.

If your Golden Retriever is demanding attention by jumping, ignore him until he has all four feet on the ground.

The moment your Golden stops the undesirable behaviour and comes towards you, you can reward his good behaviour. You can back this up by running through a couple of simple exercises, such as a Sit or a Down, and rewarding with treats. In this way, your Golden focuses his attention on you, and sees you as the greatest source of reward and pleasure.

In a more extreme situation, when you want to interrupt undesirable behaviour, and you know that a simple "No" will not do the trick, you can try something a little more dramatic. If you get a can and fill it with pebbles, it will make a really loud noise when you shake it or throw it. The same effect can be achieved with purpose-made training discs. The dog will be

startled and stop what he is doing. Even better, the dog will not associate the unpleasant noise with you. This gives you the perfect opportunity to be the nice guy, calling the dog to you and giving him lots of praise.

PROBLEM BEHAVIOUR

If you have trained your Golden from puppyhood, survived his adolescence and established yourself as a fair and consistent leader, you will end up with a brilliant companion dog. The Golden is a well-balanced dog who is biddable, eager to please, and rarely has hang-ups. Most Goldens share an exuberant love of life, and thrive on spending time with their owners.

However, problems may arise unexpectedly, or you may have taken on a rescued Golden that

has established behavioural problems. If you are worried about your Golden and feel out of your depth, do not delay in seeking professional help. This is readily available, usually through a referral from your vet, or you can find out additional information on the internet (see Appendices for web addresses). An animal behaviourist will have experience in tackling problem behaviour and will be able to help both you and your dog.

SEPARATION ANXIETY

The Golden Retriever is a wonderful companion dog who loves to be with his family; the worst scenario for a Golden is to be left for long periods. If this happens, a Golden will become bored and distressed, and is likely to be destructive. If you have to spend long periods away from home, this is not the breed for you.

Obviously, your Golden Retriever must learn to accept short periods of separation from his owner, and if he is accustomed to this from puppyhood, there is no reason why he should become anxious. A new puppy should be left for short periods on his own, ideally in a crate where he cannot get up to any mischief. It is a good idea to leave him with a boredom-busting toy (see page 83) so he will be happily occupied in your absence. When you return, do not rush to the crate and make a huge fuss. Wait a few minutes, and then calmly go to the crate and release your dog, telling him how good he has been. If this scenario is

An anxious dog is more likely to settle in a crate, where he feels safe and secure.

repeated a number of times, your Golden will soon learn that being left on his own is no big deal.

Problems with separation anxiety are most likely to arise if you take on a rescued dog who has major insecurities. You may also find that your Golden hates being left if you failed to accustom him to short periods of isolation when he was growing up. Separation anxiety is expressed in a number of ways, and all are equally upsetting for both dog and owner. An anxious dog who is left alone may bark and whine continuously, urinate and defecate, and may be extremely destructive.

There are a number of steps you can take when attempting to solve this problem.

- Put up a baby-gate between adjoining rooms and leave your dog in one room while you are in the other room. Your dog will be able to see you and hear you, but he is learning to cope without being right next to you. Build up the amount of time you can leave your dog in easy stages.
- Buy some boredom-busting toys and fill them with some tasty treats. Whenever you leave your dog, give him a food-filled toy so that he is busy while you are away.
- If you have not used a crate before, it is not too late to start. Make sure the crate is big and comfortable, and train your Golden to get used to going in his crate while you are in the same room. Gradually build up

the amount of time he spends in the crate, and then start leaving the room for short periods. When you return, do not make a fuss of your dog. Leave him for five or 10 minutes before releasing him so that he gets used to your comings and goings.
- Pretend to go out, putting on your coat and jangling keys, but do not leave the house. An anxious dog often becomes hyped up by the ritual of leave taking, and so this will help to desensitize him.
- When you go out, leave a radio or a TV on. Some dogs are comforted by hearing voices and background noise when they are left alone.
- Try to make your absences as short as possible when you are first training your dog to accept being on his own. When you

return, do not fuss your dog, rushing to his crate to release him. Leave him for a few minutes, and, when you go to him, remain calm and relaxed so that he does not become hyped up with a huge greeting.

If you take these steps, your dog should become less anxious, and, over a period of time, you should be able to solve the problem. However, if you are failing to make progress, do not delay in calling in expert help.

DOMINANCE
If you have trained and socialised your Golden correctly, he will know his place in the family pack and will have no desire to challenge your authority. As we have seen, adolescent dogs test the boundaries, and this is the time to enforce all your earlier

Sometimes a dog will seek to elevate his status by challenging house rules.

training so your Golden accepts that he is not top dog.

Goldens were bred to be biddable, so it is rare for a Golden to be over-assertive. However, if you have taken on a rescued dog who has not been trained and socialised, or if you have let your adolescent Golden rule the roost, you may find you have problems with a dominant dog. In most cases, dominance tends to be more of a problem in male dogs.

Dominance is expressed in many different ways, which may include the following:

Teach your dog to "Wait" at doorways, allowing you to go through first.

- Showing lack of respect for your personal space. For example, your dog will barge through doors ahead of you or jump up at you.
- Getting up on to the sofa or your favourite armchair, and growling when you tell him to get back on the floor.
- Becoming possessive over a toy, or guarding his food bowl by growling when you get too close.
- Growling when anyone approaches his bed or when anyone gets too close to where he is lying.
- Ignoring basic obedience commands.
- Showing no respect to younger members of the family, pushing amongst them and completely ignoring them.
- Male dogs may start marking (cocking their leg) in the house.
- Aggression towards people (see page 109).

If you see signs of your Golden becoming too dominant, you must work at lowering his status so that he realises that you are the leader and he must accept your authority. Although you need to be firm, you also need to use positive training methods so that your Golden is rewarded for the behaviour you want. In this way, his 'correct' behaviour will be strengthened and repeated.

There are a number of steps you can take to lower your Golden's status. They include:
- Go back to basics and hold daily training sessions. Make

sure you have some really tasty treats, or find a toy your Golden really values and only bring it out at training sessions. Run through all the training exercises you have taught your Golden. Make a big fuss of him and reward him when he does well. This will reinforce the message that you are the leader and that it is rewarding to do as you ask.
- Teach your Golden something new; this can be as simple as learning a trick, such as shaking paws. Having something new to think about will mentally stimulate your Golden, and he will benefit from interacting with you.
- Be 100 per cent consistent with all house rules – your Golden must never sit on the sofa, and you must never allow him to jump up at you.
- If your Golden is becoming possessive over toys, remove all his toys and keep them out of reach. Periodically, you can allow him to play with a toy, but make sure you are supervising the play session. For example, play a retrieve game so that your Golden brings the toy back to you. At the end of the play session, swap the toy with a treat and reward your Golden for giving up the toy. In time, your Golden will learn that you 'own' the toys and he will respect your authority.
- If your Golden has been guarding his food bowl, put the bowl down empty, and drop in a little food at a time.

AGGRESSION

ggression is a complex issue, as there are different causes and the behaviour may be triggered by numerous factors. It may be directed towards people, but far more commonly it is directed towards other dogs. Aggression in dogs may be the result of:

- Dominance (see page 107).
- Defensive behaviour: This may be induced by fear, pain or punishment.
- Territory: A dog may become aggressive if strange dogs or people enter his territory (which is generally seen as the house and garden).
- Intra-sexual issues: This is aggression between sexes – male-to-male or female-to-female.
- Parental instinct: A mother dog may become aggressive if she is protecting her puppies.

A dog who has been well socialised (see page 100) and has been given sufficient exposure to other dogs at significant stages of his development will rarely be aggressive. A well-bred Golden that has been reared correctly should not have a hint of aggression in his temperament. Obviously if you have taken on an older, rescued dog, you will have little or no knowledge of his background, and if he shows signs of aggression, the cause will need to be determined. In most cases, you would be well advised to call in professional help if you see aggressive behaviour in your dog; if the aggression is directed towards people, you should seek immediate advice. This behaviour can escalate very quickly and could lead to disastrous consequences.

Periodically stop dropping in the food, and tell your Golden to "Sit" and "Wait". Give it a few seconds, and then reward him by dropping in more food. This shows your Golden that you are the provider of the food, and he can only eat when you allow him to.

- Make sure the family eats before you feed your Golden. Some trainers advocate eating in front of the dog (maybe just a few bites from a biscuit) before starting a training session, so the dog appreciates your elevated status.
- Do not let your Golden barge

through doors ahead of you or leap from the back of the car before you release him. You may need to put your dog on the lead and teach him to "Wait" at doorways, and then reward him for letting you go through first.

If your Golden is progressing well with his retraining programme, think about getting involved with a dog sport, such as agility or competitive obedience. This will give your Golden a positive outlet for his energies. However, if your Golden is still seeking to be dominant, or you have any other

concerns, do not delay in seeking the help of an animal behaviourist.

NEW CHALLENGES
If you enjoy training your Golden, you may want to try one of the many dog sports that are now on offer.

GOOD CITIZEN SCHEME
This is a scheme run by the Kennel Club in the UK and the American Kennel Club in the USA. The schemes promote responsible ownership and help you to train a well-behaved dog who will fit in with the

community. The schemes are excellent for all pet owners, and they are also a good starting point if you plan to compete with your Golden when he is older. The KC and the AKC schemes vary in format. In the UK there are three levels: bronze, silver and gold, with each test becoming progressively more demanding. In the AKC scheme there is a single test.

Some of the exercises include:

- Walking on a loose lead among people and other dogs.
- Recall amid distractions.
- A controlled greeting where dogs stay under control while owners meet.
- The dog allows all-over grooming and handling by his owner and also accepts being handled by the examiner.
- Stays, with the owner in sight and then out of sight.
- Food manners, allowing the owner to eat without begging, and taking a treat on command.
- Sendaway – sending the dog to his bed.

The tests are designed to show the control you have over your dog, and his ability to respond correctly and remain calm in all situations. The Good Citizen Scheme is taught at most training clubs. For more information, log on to the Kennel Club or AKC website (see Appendices).

Showing is highly competitive, as the breed attracts large entries to classes.

SHOWING

In your eyes, your Golden is the most beautiful dog in the world – but would a judge agree? Showing is a highly competitive sport and as the Golden is so popular, classes tend to be very big. However, many owners get bitten by the showing bug, and their calendar is governed by the dates of the top showing fixtures.

To be successful in the show ring, a Golden must conform as closely as possible to the breed standard, which is a written blueprint describing the 'perfect' Golden (see Chapter 7). To get started you need to buy a puppy that has show potential and then train him to perform in the ring. A Golden will be expected to stand in show pose, gait for the judge in order to show off his natural movement, and to be examined by the judge. This involves a detailed hands-on examination, so your Golden must be bombproof when handled by strangers.

Many training clubs hold ringcraft classes, which are run by experienced showgoers. At these classes, you will learn how to handle your Golden in the ring, and you will also find out about rules, procedures and show ring etiquette.

The best plan is to start off at some small, informal shows where you can practise and learn the tricks of the trade before graduating to bigger shows. It's a long haul starting in the very first puppy class, but the dream is to make your Golden up into a Show Champion.

COMPETITIVE OBEDIENCE

Border Collies and German Shepherds dominate this sport, but gundogs have also made their mark at the highest level. Golden Retrievers have proved particularly successful, and although patience is required to achieve the level of accuracy and precision that is required, a Golden is more than capable of the task. The challenge is to motivate your dog so that he wants to work for you, and to keep training sessions light-hearted so that your Golden is always having fun. In competition, classes start off being relatively easy and become progressively more challenging, with additional exercises and the handler giving minimal instructions to the dog.

Exercises include:

- **Heelwork:** Dog and handler must complete a set pattern on and off the lead, which includes left turns, right turns, about turns, and changes of pace.
- **Recall:** This may be when the handler is stationary or on the move.
- **Retrieve:** This may be a dumbbell or any article chosen by the judge.
- **Sendaway:** The dog is sent to a designated spot and must go into an instant Down until he is recalled by the handler.
- **Stays:** The dog must stay in the Sit and in the Down for a set amount of time. In advanced classes, the hander is out of sight.
- **Scent:** The dog must retrieve

Goldens love to work closely with their owner and enjoy the challenge of competitive obedience.

a single cloth from a pre-arranged pattern of cloths that has his owner's scent, or, in advanced classes, the judge's scent. There may also be decoy cloths.

- **Distance control:** The dog must execute a series of moves (Sit, Stand, Down) without moving from his position and with the handler at a distance.

Even though competitive obedience requires accuracy and precision, make sure it is fun for your Golden, with lots of praise and rewards so that you motivate him to do his best. Many training clubs run advanced classes for those who want to compete in obedience, or you can hire the services of a professional trainer for one-on-one sessions.

AGILITY

This fun sport has grown enormously in popularity over the past few years. If you fancy having a go, make sure you have good control over your Golden and keep him slim. Agility is a very physical sport, which demands fitness from both dog and handler. A fat Golden is never going to make it as an agility competitor. Goldens are not as fast as some breeds, such as the Border Collie, but they can make up for this by being neat and accurate, and responding instantly to commands.

In agility competitions, each dog must complete a set course over a series of obstacles, which include:

- Jumps (upright hurdles and long jump)
- Weaves
- A-frame
- Dog walk
- Seesaw
- Tunnels (collapsible and rigid)
- Tyre

Dogs may compete in Jumping classes with jumps, tunnels and weaves, or in Agility classes, which have the full set of equipment. Faults are awarded for poles down on the jumps, missed contact points on the A-frame, dog walk and seesaw, and refusals. If a dog takes the wrong course, he is eliminated. The winner is the dog that completes the course in the fastest time with no faults. As you progress up the levels, courses become progressively harder with more twists, turns and changes of direction.

If you want to get involved in agility, you will need to find a club that specialises in the sport (see Appendices). You will not be allowed to start training until your Golden is 12 months old, and you cannot compete until he is 18 months old. This rule is for the protection of the dog, who may suffer injury if he puts strain on bones and joints while he is still growing.

FIELD TRIALS

This is a sport where the Golden excels, as it tests his natural working ability. There is now a split between working Goldens and show Goldens, and if you are interested in competing in field trials, you will need a Golden that is bred from working lines.

In field trials, dogs are trained to work in an entirely natural

It takes patience and dedication to compete at the top level in field trials.

AGILITY STARS
The athletic Golden Retriever makes his mark in agility.

Clearing the hurdles...

Negotiating the seesaw...

Soaring across the long jump...

Powering through the tunnel.

The Golden Retriever is a natural worker, combining athleticism, a waterproof coat – and the brains to do the job.

environment. Nothing is set up, staged or artificial. The dogs may be asked to retrieve shot game from any type of terrain, including swamp, thick undergrowth and from water. They also need to perform blind retrieves, where they are sent out to find shot game when they haven't seen it fall. Dogs are judged on their natural game-finding abilities, their work in the shooting field, and their response to their handler. The two most crucial elements are steadiness and obedience.

Goldens are built for this demanding job, with their waterproof coat, athletic physique and their great swimming ability. The other great plus factor is that Goldens love to work closely with their handlers, so, if you put in the training, you could get to the top levels and even make your Golden

into a Field Trial Champion.

If you are not aiming for the dizzy heights of making up a Field Trial Champion, you can test your Golden's working ability with the Gundog Working Certificate, which examines basic hunting and retrieving skills in the field. There is also a test designed for show dogs who must prove they have working ability in order to become a full Champion, rather than a Show Champion.

WORKING TRIALS
This is a very challenging sport, but the Golden, with his excellent sense of smell, can be very successful. The sport consists of three basic components:

• **Control:** Dog and handler must complete obedience exercises, but the work does not have to be as precise as it is in

competitive obedience. In the advanced classes, manwork (where the dog works as a guard/protection dog) is a major feature.
• **Agility:** The dog must negotiate a 3 ft (0.91 m) hurdle, a 9 ft (2.75 m) long jump, and a 6 ft (1.82) upright scale, which is the most taxing piece of dog equipment.
• **Nosework:** The dog must follow a track that has been laid over a set course. The surface may vary, and the length of time between the track being laid and the dog starting work is increased in the advanced classes.

The ladder of stakes are: Companion Dog, Utility Dog, Working Dog, Tracking Dog and Patrol Dog. In the US, tracking is a sport in its own right, and is

Your Golden Retriever will appreciate the quality time you spend with him.

very popular among Golden owners.

If you want to get involved in working trials, you will need to find a specialist club or a trainer that specialises in training for working trials. For more information, see Appendices.

FLYBALL

Goldens are natural retrievers, so they can be easily trained to be flyball competitors. Flyball is a team sport; the dogs love it, and it is undoubtedly the nosiest of all the canine sports!

Four dogs are selected to run in a relay race against an opposing team. The dogs are sent out by their handlers to jump four hurdles, catch the ball from the flyball box, and then return over the hurdles. At the top level, this sport is fast and furious, and although it is dominated by Border Collies, reliable Goldens can make a big

contribution. This is particularly true in multi-breed competitions where the team is made up of four dogs of different breeds, and only one can be a Border Collie or a Working Sheepdog. Points are awarded to dogs and teams. Annual awards are given to top dogs and top teams, and milestone awards are given out to dogs as they attain points throughout their flyballing careers.

DANCING WITH DOGS

This sport is relatively new, but it is becoming increasingly popular. It is very entertaining to watch, but it is certainly not as simple as it looks. To perform a choreographed routine to music with your Golden demands a huge amount of training.

Dancing with dogs is divided into two categories: heelwork to

music and canine freestyle. In heelwork to music, the dog must work closely with his handler and show a variety of close 'heelwork' positions. In canine freestyle, the routine can be more flamboyant, with the dog working at a distance from the handler and performing spectacular tricks. Routines are judged on style and presentation, content and accuracy.

SUMMING UP

The Golden is one of the most popular companion dogs in the world, and deservedly so. He has an outstanding temperament, and he is fun and rewarding to live with. Make sure you keep your half of the bargain: spend time socialising and training your Golden so that you can be proud to take him anywhere, and he will always be a credit to you.

THE PERFECT GOLDEN RETRIEVER

Chapter 7

The Breed Standard for the Golden Retriever was first compiled by the Golden Retriever Club, under the auspices of Mrs Charlesworth, in 1911. It was then submitted to, and accepted by, the Kennel Club in that year, where the breed was classified as 'Golden or Yellow Retriever'. The content of the original Standard differed from that of today's version on a number of points. It depended on the allocation of points for each of the 10 listed features, with a maximum of 115 points for a 'perfect' Golden on the day. It's interesting to note that, in 1910, one year prior to the Breed Standard being devised and accepted, there were eight Golden or Yellow Retrievers entered at Crufts. In 1932 the Crufts entry went into three figures and in 2007 there were 691 entries, making the Golden Retriever the highest entry in the Gundog Group at Crufts.

THE ORIGINAL UK GOLDEN RETRIEVER BREED STANDARD (1911)

GENERAL APPEARANCE
The dog should appear symmetrical, active and powerful, with a good level movement. He should be sound and well put together, with a kindly expression, without being clumsy or long in the leg.

HEAD (MAX 20 POINTS)
The skull should be broad, and well set on a clean and muscular neck. The muzzle should be powerful and wide, not weak-jawed, good stop.
The dog's eyes must be dark, and set well apart, with dark rims and a very kindly expression.
The teeth should be even, neither under nor overshot.

EARS (MAX FIVE POINTS)
Well proportioned, of moderate size and well set on.

NOSE (MAX FIVE POINTS)
The nose should be black, but a light-coloured one should not debar a dog from honours who is good in all other respects.

COLOUR (MAX FIVE POINTS)
The rich golden colour must not be as dark as the Irish Setter, equally the dog should not be cream coloured. The presence of a few white hairs on chest or toes is permissible. (White collar or blaze to be penalized.)

COAT (MAX FIVE POINTS)
The coat should be flat or wavy; with good feathering, and dense, water resisting undercoat.

FEET (MAX 10 POINTS)
The feet should be round and cat-like, not open or splay.

It is vital that the Breed Standard reflects the Golden Retriever's original role as a working gundog.

FORELEGS (MAX 10 POINTS)
Forelegs must be straight, with good bone.

HIND-LEGS (MAX 10 POINTS)
The hind-legs should be strong and muscular, with well bent stifles. Hocks must be well let down, but not cow-hocked.

TAIL (MAX FIVE POINTS)
The tail should not be carried too gay or curled at tip.

BODY (MAX 25 POINTS)
The body should be well-balanced, short coupled and deep through the heart. Loins should be strong, with deep, and well sprung ribs. Shoulders should be well laid back and long in the blade.

NOTE
The average weight for dogs in good hard condition should be:

Dogs: 65-70 lb Bitches: 56-60 lb
The height at the shoulder should be: Dogs: 23-24 in; Bitches: 20.5-22 in.

STRIVING FOR PERFECTION

Breeders continually strive to breed the 'perfect' Golden Retriever, and although some dogs come very close to perfection, we must assume that the ultimate has not yet been achieved. We must continue to breed dogs that conform as closely as possible to our Kennel Club's Breed Standard, as well as supporting the health-screening initiatives for the breed. Currently, all breeding stock should, as a minimal requirement, have their eyes checked and hips X-rayed under the BVA schemes (see Chapter 8). However, we as breeders must get our priorities right and ensure

that, within reason, we retain temperament and type, too.

Everyone with a purebred dog will have looked at his pedigree, but many people are not fully aware of just what the pedigree is trying to portray. To the average person it is just a list of names – some in red ink if you are lucky – with no further meaning. With a little research, it is possible to find and scrutinise the photographs of your dog's ancestors and see how closely they compare with your own Golden. To the experienced breeder or owner the pedigree is a guide to portraying type, and how the dog should look, as well as the qualities and traits he should possess. This is not always the case, as every mating is individual and things do not always go to plan, but we must all continue to strive to maintain the correct temperament and type.

KENNEL CLUB BREED STANDARD CHANGES

1936

Colour: The point on colour was changed to read: "Any shade of gold or cream, but neither red nor mahogany. The presence of a few white hairs on chest permissible. White collar, feet, toes or blaze to be penalised."

Size: There was also a change in the required height of the Golden. It became 22-24 inches for dogs and 20-22 inches for bitches.

1940

Nose: The following point was amended or added to read: "Nose should be black."

Mouth: This point was changed to read: "Teeth should be sound and strong. Neither undershot nor overshot, the lower teeth just behind but touching the upper teeth."

1985

The Breed Standard of the Golden Retriever remained very much the same until the Kennel Club reviewed it again in 1985. On this occasion the Kennel Club dropped the ideal weights of the Golden and included points to cover characteristics, temperament and gait/movement.

1988

The Breed Standard was amended to read: "Nose preferably black." This is the Standard to which we all currently adhere.

2008

Reponding to widespread public concern about the health of pure bred dogs, the Kennel Club introduced the following introductory paragraph to all its Breed Standards:

"A Breed Standard is the guideline which describes the ideal characteristics, temperament and appearance of a breed and ensures that the breed is fit for function. Absolute soundness is essential. Breeders and judges should at all times be careful to avoid obvious conditions or exaggerations which would be detrimental in any way to the health, welfare or soundness of this breed. From time to time certain conditions or exaggerations may be considered to have the potential to affect dogs in some breeds adversely, and judges and breeders are requested to refer to the Kennel Club website for details of any such current issues. If a feature or quality is desirable it should only be present in the right measure."

It is important to look at the actual role played by the Breed Standard in the breeding, showing and judging of the Golden Retriever and how some very relevant points can be open to personal interpretation. It has been suggested that the Kennel Club Breed Standard for the Golden Retriever is far too concise and does not give enough detail on many of the salient points. It is wide open to differing interpretation. The Breed Standard should describe the dog in adequate detail, to enable the reader to form a mental picture of the ideal Golden.

All pedigree dogs are recognised by the world's three major governing bodies: the Kennel Club (KC), the American Kennel Club (AKC), and the Federation Cynologique Internationale (FCI), all of which have a Breed Standard for the Golden Retriever. The Breed Standard is the 'blueprint' to which all breeds are compared, when shown in their appropriate countries; the Standard verbally illustrates all aspects of the breed in question, from nose to tail.

There are differences between the UK and USA Breed Standards, but we will look more closely at these later in the chapter. The current AKC Standard still retains echoes of the original Kennel Club Standard of 1911. The FCI Golden Retriever Breed Standard for Europe is much the same as the Kennel Club version, so we will concentrate on both the similarities and differences of the UK and USA versions.

The Breed Standard is a very important tool when assessing the type, conformation and general appearance of the Golden Retriever and we must all aim to breed dogs that conform as closely as possible to it. Breeders should all aspire to produce dogs that not only conform to the Breed Standard, but are also healthy, both in body and mind, and are able to perform the tasks for which the Golden Retriever was originally bred.

The UK Breed Standard for the Golden Retriever is not as comprehensive as the AKC Standard and it does leave an awful lot of its detail to the individual's own interpretation. This is why you see dogs of varying colour, head shape, balance, and, in certain instances, angulation winning in the show ring. Successful show winners can vary from one Championship show to the next – not only in colour, but also in general conformation. However, they should all be within the parameters of the Breed Standard, allowing for the fact that the individual judge's subjective interpretation of the Standard's points can vary within accepted limits.

Judges must concentrate on the Breed Standard, adhere to its content, and ensure that we do not continue to see the changes in breed type that have crept upon us over the last 30 years or so. Dogs have gradually become shorter in the leg, broader in the head, and very much lighter in colour. There are now two definite types of Golden – the show type and the working type – and it must be said that the American-type Golden is, in many instances, similar to the British Golden of 30 years ago. The typical US Golden Retriever tends to be of a darker golden colour than his UK counterpart; his head is generally narrower, and he looks more like the current UK working type of Golden. To a certain extent, this pattern has changed over recent years, as more UK imports have entered North America and left their mark with breeders and exhibitors alike.

Type and temperament are of the utmost importance, but potential breeding stock must also go through health screening tests to protect future generations.

THE JUDGE'S EXAMINATION
Every dog in the ring is given a full 'hands-on' examination by the judge.

The judge will assess the head, also checking dentition.

Moving along the dog to evaluate the forequarters.

Working round to the rear of the dog.

However, the US breed type is still, generally, distinguishable from the UK counterparts. Many British post-war bloodlines are now well established in the USA and Canada, and this can be seen as the cause of a gradual change to lighter-coloured and slightly heavier-bodied Golden Retrievers that have recently emerged in some kennels.

As you study the two Standards, you will notice that there are still similarities between the American Kennel Club Breed Standard and the original Kennel Club Breed Standard, as introduced in 1911. This original Standard was used in the States until the 1950s. In the early 1950s it went through a slight revision, and then a completely new, revamped Standard was introduced in 1954. This was when the show judge was asked to disqualify for: size deviations above or below the Standard, undershot or overshot jaws, or if the dog

suffered from the myriad of eye problems listed in the Standard. This Standard was revised in 1980, and again, along with all AKC Breed Standards, in 1990. This is the Golden Retriever Breed Standard in use today. There are many variations between the KC and AKC Breed Standards; some are relatively minor, and some are more inclined to cause consternation.

INTERPRETATION AND ANALYSIS
A comparison of the UK Kennel Club and American Kennel Club Breed Standards

GENERAL APPEARANCE
KC
Symmetrical, balanced, active, powerful, level mover; sound with kindly expression. Characteristics: Biddable, intelligent and possessing natural working ability. Temperament: Kindly, friendly and confident.

AKC
A symmetrical, powerful, active dog, sound and well put together, not clumsy nor long in the leg, displaying a kindly expression and possessing a personality that is eager, alert and self-confident. Primarily a hunting dog, he should be shown in hard working condition. Overall appearance, balance, gait and purpose to be given more emphasis than any of his component parts. Faults – Any departure from the described ideal shall be considered faulty to the degree to which it interferes with the breed's purpose or is contrary to breed character.

Essentially, the Golden Retriever is a working dog, so his overall construction must be suitable for the job he was first bred to do. The AKC Standard is much more detailed in the General Appearance section than the KC version, which states only: "Symmetrical, balanced, active, powerful, level mover; sound with kindly expression". The AKC, however, also demands: "eager, alert and in hard working condition" and the "overall appearance, balance, gait and purpose" to be given more emphasis than any component part". The AKC states "not clumsy or long in the leg" – it could be advantageous if the UK Standard added "not short in the leg", as we do seem to be losing the height required to maintain balance. This heading also includes some of the requirements that come under the Characteristics and Temperament sections of the KC Standard. Balance is mentioned in both Standards, and, to the untrained eye, can be difficult to define. To the experienced eye, a balanced dog of sound construction is immediately noticeable. Balance does tend to come with maturity, so it is important not to be too critical of younger dogs who do not appear quite symmetrical in their first year or so. Requirements such as intelligence and a biddable nature are difficult to define or assess in the show ring; the judge has very little time with each exhibit and will concentrate, in the main, on temperament, construction, balance, soundness and overall ring presence.

SIZE
KC
Height at withers: Dogs: 56-61 cm (22-24 inches); Bitches: 51-56 cm (20-22 inches)

AKC
Proportion, Substance: Males 23-24 inches in height at withers; females 21.5-22.5 inches. Dogs up to one inch above or below standard size should be proportionately penalized. Deviation in height of more than one inch from the standard shall disqualify. Length from breastbone to point of buttocks slightly greater than height at withers in a ratio of 12:11. Weight for dogs 65 to 75 pounds; bitches 55 to 65 pounds.

The AKC insists on disqualification for any deviation of more than one inch over or under the Standard heights and

also for an incorrect bite. The KC does not suggest such action by a judge, just that any departure from the Standard "should be considered by the seriousness of the fault and should be regarded in exact proportion to its degree". The AKC Standard gives some guidance to the required proportions and, ultimately, toward a more balanced dog.

HEAD AND SKULL
KC
Balanced and well chiselled, skull broad without coarseness; well set on neck, muzzle powerful, wide and deep. Length of foreface approximately equals length from well-defined stop to

The skull is broad and well chiselled.

The Golden's Retriever should have a scissor bite, with the teeth on the upper jaw closely overlapping the teeth on the lower jaw.

occiput. Nose preferably black.
Eyes: Dark brown, set well apart, dark rims.
Ears: Moderate size, set on approximate level with eyes.
Mouth: Jaws strong, with perfect, regular and complete scissor bite, i.e. upper teeth closely overlapping lower teeth and set square to the jaws.

AKC
Head: Broad in skull, slightly arched laterally and longitudinally without prominence of frontal bones (forehead) or occipital bones. Stop well defined but not abrupt. Foreface deep and wide, nearly as long as skull.
Muzzle: Straight in profile, blending smooth and strongly into skull; when viewed in profile or from above, slightly deeper and wider at stop than at tip. No heaviness in flews. Removal of whiskers is permitted but not preferred.
Eyes: Friendly and intelligent in expression, medium large and dark, close fitting rims, set well apart and reasonably deep in sockets. Color preferably dark brown; medium brown acceptable. Slant eyes and narrow, triangular eyes detract from correct expression and are to be faulted. No white or haw visible when looking straight ahead. Dogs showing evidence of functional abnormality of eyelids or eyelashes (such as, but not limited to, trichiasis, entropion, ectropion, or distichiasis) are to be excused from the ring.

Ears: Rather short with front edge attached well behind and just above the eye and falling close to cheek. When pulled forward, tip of ear should just cover the eye. Low, hound-like ear set to be faulted. Nose black or brownish black, though fading to a lighter shade in cold weather not serious. Pink nose or nose seriously lacking in pigmentation to be faulted.
Teeth: scissors bite, in which the outer side of the lower incisors touches the inner side of the upper incisors. Undershot or overshot bite is a disqualification. Misalignment of teeth (irregular placement of incisors) or a level bite (incisors meet each other edge to edge) is undesirable, but not to be confused with undershot or overshot. Full dentition. Obvious gaps are a serious fault.

The head is covered in adequate detail in both Standards, although there is a variation in wording. First and foremost, it should be simple, visually, to identify a male or female adult Golden Retriever solely from the head shape and size. The Standard requires a head to be 'balanced and well-chiselled', this is most important, as a lack of chiselling gives the head an undesirable heavy or cloddy appearance. It has become, in some instances, difficult to define the sex of the Golden, as 'doggy-headed' bitches and 'bitchy-headed' dogs are becoming more prevalent in the show ring. This is a fault and it must be treated as such.

The AKC is much more descriptive concerning the eyes. It is crucial that we maintain the correct eye in the Golden Retriever, as it is the major contributor to the breed's melting expression. A dark eye with dark pigmented rims are desirable, because any other, lighter, eye colour looks unnatural, which spoils the whole character of the head. The AKC Standard covers the same salient points, but adds much more detail and guidance, particularly in what is not required.

Ear size and set is covered adequately in both Standards, with emphasis on moderate size and correct placement. Currently, there is some variation, both in shape and size of the ears of the Golden, and this does become evident when seen on the move. The ears should be set so that the front edge is level with the eye; high- or low-set ears destroy the required expression.

The Golden Retriever's nose should be "preferably black". The AKC Standard expands on this point by adding "black or brownish black" and "pink nose or nose seriously lacking in pigmentation to be faulted". I think all would agree that a Golden's overall appearance is much improved by a black nose.

The mouth of the Golden Retriever should be both soft and strong, as it is a bird-carrying dog and these elements are crucial for him to fulfil this task successfully. Both Standards agree on the required scissor bite; however, the AKC Standard advocates disqualification for either undershot or overshot mouths, and requires the full dentition of 42 teeth, with obvious gaps to be faulted. The dentition issue tends to be treated more severely in the US than in the UK.

NECK AND BODY
KC
Neck: Good length, clean and muscular.
Body: Balanced, short-coupled, deep through the heart. Ribs deep, well sprung. Level top line.

Tail: Set on and carried level with back, reaching to hocks, without curl at tip.

AKC
Neck, Top line, Body: Neck medium long, merging gradually into well laid back shoulders, giving sturdy, muscular appearance. No throatiness. Back line strong and level from withers to slightly sloping croup, whether standing or moving. Sloping back line, roach or sway back to be faulted. Body well balanced, short coupled, deep through chest. Chest between forelegs at least as wide as a man's closed hand including thumb, with

The typical friendly, intelligent expression of the Golden Retriever reflected in dark brown eyes.

The body is short coupled with a level topline.

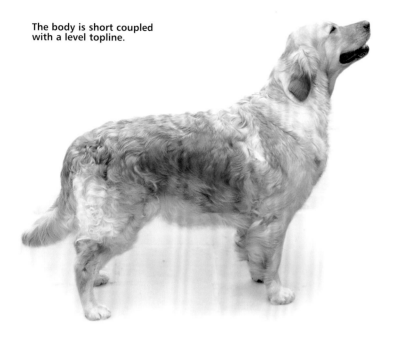

FOREQUARTERS AND FEET
KC

Forequarters: Forelegs straight with good bone, shoulders well laid back, long in blade with upper arm of equal length placing legs well under body. Elbows close fitting.
Feet: Round and cat-like.

AKC

Forequarters: Muscular, well coordinated with hindquarters and capable of free movement. Shoulder blades long and well laid back with upper tips fairly close together at withers. Upper arms appear about the same length as the blades, setting the elbows back beneath the upper tip of the blades, close to the ribs without looseness. Legs, viewed from the front, straight with good bone, but not to the point of coarseness. Pasterns short and strong, sloping slightly with no suggestion of weakness. Dewclaws on forelegs may be removed but are normally left on.
Feet: Feet medium size, round, compact and well knuckled, with thick pads. Excess hair may be trimmed to show natural size and contour. Splayed or hare feet to be faulted.

well developed fore chest. Brisket extends to elbow. Ribs long and well-sprung but not barrel shaped, extending well towards hindquarters. Loin short, muscular, wide and deep, with very little tuck-up. Slab-sidedness, narrow chest, lack of depth in brisket, excessive tuck-up to be faulted. Tail well set on, thick and muscular at the base, following the natural line of the croup. Tail bones extend to, but not below, the point of hock. Carried with merry action, level or with some moderate upward curve; never curled over back nor between legs.

The body is arguably the greatest contributor to the overall picture of the Golden Retriever. All parts need to be in proportion with each other, to emphasise balance. The dog's length to height ratio is crucial, as is his depth of chest through the ribs. The dog's coupling (or loin) should be short, and the ribs should be felt but not seen, and should be well sprung, but not barrelled or slab-sided. Both the UK and the US Standards require a level top line, deep, well sprung ribs and a short-coupled body, with the tail well set on and just reaching the hocks.

The neck, top line and body are defined well in both Standards, with just a difference in vocabulary. Both Standards require a good reach of neck, with no throatiness. The neck should be strong and muscular, merging into well-placed shoulders, to contribute to the overall balance. The AKC is, once again, more descriptive in detail.

Forequarters are covered well, although more explicitly in the AKC than the KC Standard. The AKC highlights points viewed from the front of the dog, requiring front legs to be "straight with good bone" and the pasterns "short and strong". The

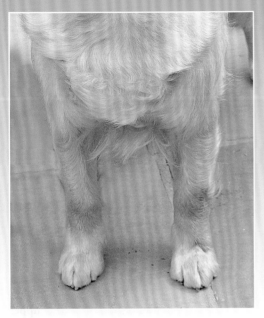

The forelegs are straight, showing good bone.

The hindquarters are strong and muscular.

most important aspect of the Golden Retriever's forequarters is shoulder angulation, length of shoulder blade (scapula), and an equal length of the upper arm. The AKC states that a 90-degree angle is required between the scapula and humerus (the shoulder blade and the upper arm). Unfortunately, this point is omitted from the UK Standard, although breeders and judges alike do look for this important factor in the breed. Without good front construction, the dog's balance and movement will be incorrect. Poor or faulty fronts are difficult to breed out and can involve many generations of disappointing conformation. The

Standard also requires a straight front, with legs that are not bowed or out at the elbow; nor should the elbows be 'loose'. Strong pasterns act as nature's shock absorbers and are essential for a dog to move and jump correctly for prolonged periods.

The Golden Retriever's feet should be "round and cat-like". This point is evident, although not word for word, in both Standards. The AKC continues to advocate trimming to enhance the "natural size and contour" of the feet and emphasises the point that "splayed or hare feet" should be faulted. The removal of dewclaws is allowed, but they are usually left on.

HINDQUARTERS
KC
Hindquarters: Loin and legs strong and muscular, good second thighs, well-bent stifles. Hocks well let down, straight when viewed from rear, neither turning in nor out. Cow-hocks highly undesirable.

AKC
Hindquarters: Broad and strongly muscled. Profile of croup slopes slightly; the pelvic bone slopes at a slightly greater angle (approximately 30 degrees from horizontal). In a natural stance, the femur joins the pelvis at approximately a 90 degree angle; stifles well bent;

hocks well let down with short, strong rear pasterns. Feet as in front. Legs straight when viewed from the rear. Cow-hocks, spread hocks and sickle hocks to be faulted.

The hindquarters are perhaps the most important anatomical part of the Golden Retriever's structure, stance and movement, and should mirror the angulation and balance of the forequarters. The AKC states a required angle between the pelvis and femur of 90 degrees. Although this is not mentioned in the UK Standard, all those familiar with the breed would agree on this point. The correct rear angulation or 'turn of stifle' is certainly desirable, as this is the Golden Retriever's "engine"; the source of its power and drive.

Both Standards agree that straight hocks are desired and cow-hocks should be faulted. Generally, if the dog has good hocks, then movement will be improved accordingly. There is a tendency in the ring today for Golden Retrievers to move poorly or incorrectly. This problem may be caused by over-angulation, moving close behind, or just lack of muscle power.

TAIL
KC
Tail: Set on and carried level with back, reaching top hocks, without curl at tip.

AKC
Tail: Tail well set on, thick and muscular at the base, following a natural line of the croup. Tail bone extends to, but not below, the point of hock. Carried with merry action, level or with some moderate upward curve; never curled over back nor between the legs.

The KC Standard is quite brief in its requirement for the tail – whereas the AKC is somewhat more explicit in its demands. The tail is a very important part of the dog's overall balance and conformation and can so easily spoil the whole picture if it is too long, curved or carried 'gay' and should be penalised accordingly.

COAT
KC
Coat: Flat or wavy with good feathering, dense water-resisting undercoat.

The full range of Golden Retriever colours from dark to light.

AKC

Coat: Dense and water-repellent with good undercoat. Outer coat firm and resilient, neither coarse nor silky, lying close to body; may be straight or wavy. Untrimmed natural ruff; moderate feathering on back of forelegs and on under body; heavier feathering on front of neck, back of thighs and underside of tail. Coat on head, paws and front of legs is short and even. Excessive length, open coats, and limp, soft coats are very undesirable. Feet may be trimmed and stray hairs neatened, but the natural appearance of coat or outline should not be altered by cutting or clipping.

Both Standards require a dense, water-repellent undercoat with a flat (straight) or wavy top coat. The AKC Standard expands in detail what may be trimmed without altering the natural outline of the Golden. The profuse coat is perhaps one of the Golden Retriever's greatest visual attributes to the untrained eye, and a gleaming, golden coat in the sunlight is very attractive.

COLOUR
KC

Colour: Any shade of gold or cream, neither red nor mahogany. A few white hairs, on chest only, permissible.

AKC

Color: Rich, lustrous golden of various shades. Feathering may be lighter than rest of the coat.

With the exception of graying or whitening of face or body due to age, any white marking, other than a few white hairs on the chest, should be penalised according to its extent. Allowable light shadings are not to be confused with white markings. Predominant body color which is either extremely pale or extremely dark is undesirable. Some latitude should be given to the light puppy whose coloring shows promise of deepening with maturity. Any noticeable area of black or other off-color hair is a serious fault.

Coat colour is a very subjective issue. The 'in-colour' does seem to change from time to time in the

The judge will assess movement from the front, the rear and from the side.

UK. The North American scene appears a little more stable, with its darker golden shades, although some UK breeding seems to be influencing some kennels. Colour is a point where the Standards differ; the KC asks for "any shade of gold or cream, neither red nor mahogany" whereas the AKC asks for "a rich, lustrous golden coat of various shades."

MOVEMENT
KC
Gait/Movement: Powerful with good drive. Straight and true in front and rear. Stride long and free with no sign of hackney action in front.

AKC
Gait: When trotting, gait is free, smooth, powerful and well coordinated, showing good reach. Viewed from any position, legs turn neither in nor out, nor do feet cross or interfere with each other. As speed increases, feet tend to converge toward center line of

balance. It is recommended that dogs be shown on a loose lead to reflect true gait.

Gait and movement are well covered in both Standards. The KC insists on a free, powerful, smooth gait with drive, while the AKC suggests the moving of the dog on a loose lead. This is something that could be practised with more effect in the UK show ring. The AKC Standard illustrates how the dog's feet converge toward a central line, as the speed of movement increases.

CHARACTERISTICS AND TEMPERAMENT
KC
Characteristics: Biddable, intelligent and possessing natural working ability.
Temperament: Kindly, friendly and confident.

AKC
Temperament: Friendly, reliable and trustworthy.
Quarrelsomeness or hostility

towards other dogs or people in normal situations, or an unwarranted show of timidity or nervousness, is not in keeping with Golden Retriever character. Such actions should be penalized according to their significance.

Characteristics and temperament are briefly outlined in the UK Standard, whereas the AKC Standard also defines what is not required. As a gundog, biddableness, intelligence and working ability are of utmost importance in the breed. Although these attributes are impossible to assess fully in the show ring, the "kindly" expression and "kindly and confident" temperament can certainly be evident, and should be rewarded. The AKC requests that "quarrelsomeness or hostility" or "timidity or nervousness" should be penalised, according to their significance. Aggression toward the judge when being shown must not be tolerated, and any offending dog should be asked to leave the ring.

FAULTS AND DISQUALIFICATIONS
KC
Faults: Any departure from the foregoing points should be considered a fault and the seriousness with which the fault should be regarded should be in exact proportion to its degree.

AKC
Disqualifications: Deviation in height of more than one inch from Standard either way. Undershot or overshot bite.

SUMMARY
Both the KC and the AKC Standards rely on an educated judge for sensible interpretation of the Standard, and, although not stated, to be kind and gentle with the dogs and fair to the exhibitors. The judge should endeavour not to 'fault judge', but should rate the dogs according to their good points (unless it's a point for disqualification) and should be prepared to supply a written critique as required by the show society. We, as breeders, exhibitors and judges, often wonder why the Golden Retriever achieves so little in the Gundog Group at Championship shows. It could be down to the wide deviation in type, enabled by the differing interpretations of the Standard by the breed judges. It could also be the wide differences in type, height and weight, giving

The biddable temperament is a hallmark of the breed.

an inconsistent representative of the Golden Retriever from one show to the next.

Finally, the UK Standard insists on two testicles being descended into the scrotum; this point is not mentioned in the AKC Standard though I am sure, if necessary, it would be penalised by the judge if not present.

It is an eternal point of confusion as to why the major Kennel Clubs, and international breed clubs, do not establish one international Breed Standard. After all, there is only one Golden Retriever. The two Standards, KC and AKC, tend to differ slightly on a number of points, but I believe an experienced judge or breeder will interpret the same overall illustration of the breed.

HAPPY AND HEALTHY

Chapter 8

The Golden Retriever is generally a resilient, active dog. Developed originally as a gundog, the Golden Retriever has a good life-span, running into double figures, provided his needs are met. The Golden is renowned as a faithful companion and a willing friend on a non-conditional basis. He will, however, as a necessity, rely on you for food and shelter, accident prevention and medication. A healthy Golden is a tail-wagging happy dog, looking to please his owner. Many will spontaneously hunt out an item such as a favourite ball or a slipper to give to their owner when they walk in the door, to welcome them home. There are a few genetic conditions that occur in the breed, such as hip dysplasia and hereditary cataracts, which will be covered in depth later in the chapter. A major omission in the Golden's design plan was a conscience when it comes to food. This is a breed notorious for greed – there is no doubt that his head is often ruled by his stomach! Those lovely dark eyes can be so expressive and persuasive, and his brain has no concept of weight control.

ROUTINE HEALTH CARE

VACCINATION

There is currently much debate over the issue of vaccination. The timing of the final part of the initial puppy vaccination course and the frequency of subsequent booster vaccinations are both under scrutiny. An evaluation of the relative risk for each disease plays a part, depending on the local situation. Many owners think that their puppy can go out for walks as soon as he or she has had the final part of the puppy vaccination course, believing the actual vaccination is the protection. This is not the case. The rationale behind vaccination is to stimulate the immune system into producing protective antibodies, which will be triggered if the patient is subsequently exposed to that particular disease. This means that a further one or two weeks will have to pass before an effective level of protection will have developed.

Vaccines against viruses stimulate longer-lasting protection than those against bacteria, whose effect may only persist for a matter of months in some cases. There is also the possibility of an individual failing to mount a full immune response to a vaccination; although the vaccine schedule may have been followed as recommended, that particular dog remains vulnerable. An individual's level of protection against rabies, as demonstrated by the antibody titre in a blood sample, is routinely tested in the

Your puppy will need to be vaccinated to protect him from a number of infectious diseases.

UK in order to fulfil the requirements of the Pet Travel Scheme (PETS). This is not the case with other individual diseases, where, in order to gauge the need for booster vaccination or to determine the effect of a course of vaccines, your veterinary surgeon will advise a protocol based upon the vaccines available, local disease prevalence, and the lifestyle of you and your dog.

It is worth remembering that maintaining a fully effective level of immune protection against the disease appropriate to your locale is vital; these are serious diseases, which may result in the demise of your dog, and some may have the potential to be passed on to his human family (so-called zoonotic potential for transmission). This is where you will be grateful for your vet's knowledge and advice.

The American Animal Hospital Association laid down guidelines at the end of 2006 for the vaccination of dogs in North America. Core diseases were defined as distemper, adenovirus, parvovirus and rabies. So-called non-core diseases are kennel cough, Lyme disease and leptospirosis; a decision to vaccinate against one or more non-core diseases is based on an individual's level of risk, determined on lifestyle and where you live in the US.

Do remember, however, that the booster visit to the veterinary surgery is not 'just' for a booster. I am regularly correcting my clients when they announce that they have 'just' brought their pet for a booster. Instead, this appointment is a chance for a full health-check and evaluation of how your dog is doing. After all, we are all familiar with the adage that a human year is equivalent to seven canine years. There have been attempts in recent times to reset the scale for two reasons: small breeds live longer than giant breeds, and dogs are living longer than previously. I have seen dogs of 17 and 18 years of age, but to say a dog is 119 or 126 years old is plainly meaningless. It does emphasise the fact, though, that a dog's health can change dramatically over the course of a single year because dogs age at a far greater rate than humans.

For me as a veterinary surgeon, the booster vaccination visit is a challenge: how much can I find of which the owner was unaware, such as rotten teeth or a heart murmur? Even monitoring bodyweight year upon year is of use because bodyweight can creep up or down without an owner realising. Being overweight is unhealthy, but it may take an outsider's remark to make an owner realise that there is a problem. Conversely, a drop in bodyweight may be the only pointer to an underlying problem.

The diseases against which dogs are vaccinated include:

ADENOVIRUS

Canine adenovirus 1 (CAV-1) affects the liver (hepatitis) and the classic 'blue eye' appearance in some affected dogs, whilst CAV-2 is a cause of kennel cough (see later). Vaccines often include both canine adenoviruses.

DISTEMPER

This is also known as 'hardpad', from the characteristic changes to the pads of the paws. It has a worldwide distribution, but fortunately vaccination has been very effective at reducing its occurrence. It is caused by a virus and affects the respiratory, gastro-intestinal (gut) and nervous systems, so it causes a wide range of illnesses. Fox and urban stray dog populations are most at risk, and therefore responsible for local outbreaks.

The booster provides an opportunity to give a dog an annual check-up.

KENNEL COUGH (also known as INFECTIOUS TRACHEOBRONCHITIS)

Bordetella bronchiseptica is not only a major cause of kennel cough, but also a common secondary infection on top of another cause. Being a bacterium, it is susceptible to treatment with appropriate antibiotics, but the immunity stimulated by the vaccine is therefore short-lived (six to 12 months).

This vaccine is often in a form to be administered down the nostrils in order to stimulate local immunity at the point of entry, so to speak. Do not be alarmed to see your veterinary surgeon using a needle and syringe to draw up the vaccine, because the needle will be replaced with a special, plastic introducer, allowing the vaccine to be gently instilled into each nostril. Dogs generally resent being held more than the actual intra-nasal vaccine, and I have learnt that covering the patient's eyes helps greatly.

Kennel cough is, however, rather a catch-all term for any cough spreading within a dog population, not just in kennels, but also between dogs at a training session, breed show, or even mixing out in the park. Many of these infections may not be B. bronchiseptica, but other viruses, for which one can only treat symptomatically. Parainfluenza virus is often included in a vaccine programme, because it is a common viral cause of kennel cough.

Kennel cough can seem alarming. There is a persistent cough, accompanied by the production of white frothy spittle,

Kennel cough is highly contagious and will spread through a group of dogs that live together.

which can last for a matter of weeks, during which time the patient is highly infectious to other dogs. I remember when it ran through our five Border Collies – there were white patches of froth on the floor wherever you looked! Other features include sneezing, a runny nose, and eyes sore with conjunctivitis. Fortunately, these infections are generally self-limiting; most dogs recover without any long-lasting problems, but an elderly dog may be knocked sideways by it, akin to the effects of a common cold on a frail elderly person.

LEPTOSPIROSIS

This disease, also known as Weil's disease in humans, is commonly contracted through contact with rats and their urine. This is a zoonotic disease, with implications for all those in contact with an affected dog.

The UK National Rodent Survey 2003 found a wild brown rat population of 60 million,

equivalent at the time to one rat per person. I have heard it said that, in the UK, you are never more than a foot (30 cm) from a rat! This means that there is as much risk for the Golden living with a family on the edge of a town, as there is for the rural Golden, exploring ditches, ponds and farmland.

The situation in the US is less clear-cut. Blanket vaccination against leptospirosis is not considered necessary, because it only occurs in certain areas, so you must be guided by your veterinarian.

LYME DISEASE

This is a bacterial infection transmitted by hard ticks. It is therefore found in those specific areas of the US where ticks are found, such as north-eastern states, some southern states, California and the upper Mississippi region. It does also occur in the UK, but at a low level, so vaccination is not

routinely offered.

The clinical disease is manifested primarily as limping, due to arthritis, but other organs affected include the heart, kidneys and nervous system. It is readily treatable with appropriate antibiotics, once diagnosed, but the causal bacterium, Borrelia burgdorferi, is not cleared from the body totally and will persist.

Prevention requires both vaccination and tick control, especially as there are other diseases transmitted by ticks. Ticks carrying B. burgdorferi will transmit it to humans as well, but an infected dog cannot pass it to a human.

PARVOVIRUS

This virus appeared in the late 1970s, when it was thought that the UK's dog population would be decimated by it. This was a notion that terrified me at the time, but fortunately it did not happen on the scale envisaged. Occurrence is mainly low now, thanks to vaccination. It is also occasionally seen in the elderly, unvaccinated dog.

RABIES

This is another zoonotic disease and there are very strict control measures in place. Vaccines were once only available in the UK on an individual basis for dogs being taken abroad. Pets travelling into the UK had to serve six months' compulsory quarantine, so that any pet incubating rabies would be identified, before being released back into the general population. Under the Pet Travel Scheme, provided certain criteria are met, (refer to the DEFRA website for up-to-date information – www.defra.gov.uk) then dogs can re-enter the UK without being quarantined.

Dogs being imported into the US have to show that they were vaccinated against rabies at least 30 days previously; otherwise, they have to serve effective internal quarantine for 30 days from the date of the rabies vaccination in order to ensure they are not incubating rabies. The exception is dogs entering from countries recognised as being rabies-free, in which case, it has to be proved that they have lived in that country for at least six months before travelling.

PARASITES

A parasite is defined as an organism deriving benefit, on a one-way basis, from another (the host). It goes without saying that it is not to the parasite's advantage to harm the host to such an extent that the benefit is lost, especially if it results in the death of the host. This means a dog could harbour parasites, internal and/or external, without there being any signs apparent to the owner. Many canine parasites can, however, transfer to humans with variable consequences, so routine preventative treatment is advised against particular parasites. Just as with vaccination, risk assessment plays a part. For example, there is no need for routine heartworm treatment in the UK (at present), but it is vital in the US and in Mediterranean countries.

You will need to continue the worming regime started by your puppy's breeder.

INTERNAL PARASITES

ROUNDWORMS (nematodes)
Roundworms are the spaghetti-like worms that you may have been unfortunate enough to have seen passed in faeces or brought up in vomit. Most of the deworming treatments in use today cause the adults roundworms to disintegrate, thankfully, so that treating puppies in particular is not as unpleasant as it used to be!

Most puppies will have a worm burden, mainly of a particular roundworm species (*Toxocara*

canis). These worms reactivate within the dam's tissues during pregnancy and pass to the foetuses developing in the womb. Therefore, it is important to treat the dam during and after pregnancy, as well as the puppies.

Professional advice is to continue worming every month. There are roundworm eggs in the environment and, unless you examine your dog's faeces under a microscope on a very regular basis, for the presence of roundworm eggs, you will be unaware of your dog having

HEARTWORM (Dirofilaria immitis)

Heartworm infection has been diagnosed in dogs all over the world. There are two prerequisites: presence of mosquitoes and a warm, humid climate.

When a female mosquito bites an infected animal, it acquires D. immitis in its circulating form, as microfilariae. A warm temperature is needed for these microfilariae to develop into the infective third-stage – larvae (L3) – within the mosquitoes, the so-called intermediate host. L3 larvae are then transmitted by the mosquito when it next bites a dog. Therefore, while heartworm infection is found in all the states of the US, it is at differing levels. For example, an occurrence in Alaska is probably a reflection of a visiting dog, having picked up the infection elsewhere.

Until recently, heartworm infection has not been a problem in the UK except for those dogs contracting it while abroad, without suitable preventative treatment. However, global warming, and its effect on the UK's climate, has changed that and more cases are being reported.

It is a potentially life-threatening condition, which, without preventative treatment, can make dogs of all breeds and ages susceptible. The larvae can grow to 14 inches (35.5 cm) within the right side of the heart, causing primarily signs of heart failure and ultimately liver and kidney damage. It can be treated, but prevention is a better plan. In the US, regular blood tests for the presence of infection are advised, coupled with appropriate preventative measures. It is advisable to liaise with your veterinary surgeon.

For dogs travelling to heartworm-endemic areas of the EU, such as the Mediterranean coast, preventative treatment should be started before leaving the UK and maintained during the visit. Again, this is best arranged with your vet.

picked up roundworms, unless he should have such a heavy burden that he passes the adults. It takes a few weeks from the time that a dog swallows a Toxocara canis roundworm egg, to him passing viable eggs (the pre-patent period). There are deworming products that are active all the time, which will provide continuous protection when administered as directed. Otherwise, treating every month will prevent a dog becoming a source of roundworm eggs to the general population.

It is the risk to human health that is so important: T. canis roundworms will migrate within our tissues and cause all manner of problems, not least of which is blindness. If a dog has roundworms, the eggs also find their way on to his coat where they can be picked up during stroking and cuddling.

You should always carefully pick up your dog's faeces, and dispose of them appropriately, which will not only reduce the chance for environmental contamination, but also make walking more pleasant underfoot.

TAPEWORMS (cestodes)

When considering the general dog population, the primary source of the most common tapeworm species will be fleas, which can carry the eggs. Most multi-wormers will be active against these tapeworms, not because they are a hazard to human health but because it is unpleasant to see the wriggly rice-grain tapeworm segments emerging from your dog's back passage while he is lying in front of the fire, and usually when you have had guests for dinner.

There are specific requirements for treatment with praziquantel within 24 to 48 hours of return into the UK under PETS. This is to prevent the inadvertent introduction of Echinococcus multilocularis, a tapeworm carried by foxes on mainland Europe; it is transmissible to humans, causing serious, or even fatal, liver disease.

EXTERNAL PARASITES

FLEAS

There are several species of flea, which are not host specific. Not only can a dog be carrying cat and human fleas as well as dog fleas, but also the same flea treatment will kill and/or control them all (though never use treatment intended for a dog on a cat and vice versa). It is also accepted that environmental control is a vital part of the flea control programme. This is because the adult flea is only on the animal in order to have a blood meal and to breed; the remainder of the lifecycle occurs in the house, car, caravan, shed...

There is a vast array of flea control products available, with various routes of administration: collar, powder, spray, 'spot-on' or oral. Flea control needs to be applied to all pets in the house, independent of whether they leave or not, since fleas can be introduced by other pets and their human owners. Therefore, it is best to discuss your specific flea control needs with your veterinary surgeon.

TICKS

There were once said to be classic pockets of ticks in the UK, such as the New Forest and Thetford Forest, but they are actually found nationwide. The lifecycle is curious; each life stage takes a year to develop and

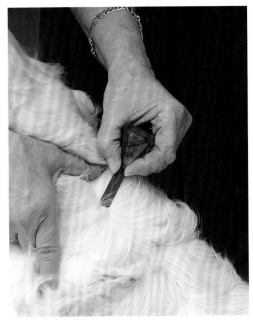

Spot-on treatment is very effective in preventing flea infestation.

move on to the next. Long grass is a major habitat; the vibration of animals moving through the grass will stimulate the larva, nymph, or adult to climb up a blade of grass and wave its legs in the air as it 'quests' for a host to latch on to for its next blood meal. Humans are as likely to be hosts as any other animal, so ramblers and orienteers are advised to cover their legs when going through rough, long grass. As well as their physical presence causing irritation, it is the potential for disease transmission that is of concern. A tick will transmit any infection previously contracted while feeding on an animal – for example, Borrelia burgdorferi, the causal agent of Lyme disease (see above).

A-Z OF COMMON AILMENTS

ACUTE MOIST DERMATITIS (AMD) or HOT SPOT

I have seen many Goldens with a patch of AMD just below the ear. The skin and overlying fur appear wet, which is due to a sticky discharge, caused by the infection in the skin. The area is very painful to the touch, meaning that it is often necessary to sedate the patient before clipping away the fur. A large area of infected skin may be revealed, but removing the fur back to visually healthy skin enables a thorough cleansing of all the affected area. A course of appropriate oral antibiotic is often prescribed, together with topical treatment. The response is generally rapid, the infection resolving within 10 to 14 days.

The initial cause may have been an insect sting or an ear infection (see below), stimulating the patient to scratch at his ear, thereby irritating the skin below it. Over the rump is another common site, thought to relate to the irritation of impacted anal sacs (see below) or fleas. Patient interference does play a role in the development of AMD and a vicious cycle establishes itself, as the infected area is itchy for the patient. Preventing further scratching and rubbing of the area is paramount for the infection to clear up.

ANAL SACS, IMPACTED

The anal sacs lie on either side of the back passage or anus at approximately four- and eight-o'-clock, if compared with the face of a clock. They fill with a particularly pungent fluid, which is emptied on to the faeces as they move past the sacs to exit from the anus. Theories abound as to why these sacs should become impacted periodically, and seemingly more so in some dogs than others. The irritation of impacted anal sacs is often seen as 'scooting', when the backside is dragged along the ground. Some dogs will gnaw at their back feet or over the rump.

Increasing the fibre content of the diet helps some dogs, although in others there could be an underlying skin disease.

However, it may be a one-off occurrence, for no apparent reason. Sometimes, an infection can become established, requiring antibiotic therapy, which may need to be coupled with flushing out the infected sac, under sedation or general anaesthesia. More rarely, a dog will present with an apparently acute-onset anal sac abscess, which is incredibly painful.

CUTANEOUS HISTIOCYTOMA

This is usually on the paws or ear flaps, but it can occur anywhere else on the body of mainly young dogs, although it can occasionally appear on middle-aged individuals. They may first be noticed as a strawberry-like growth when a few millimetres wide, which may grow to 10 or 15

millimetres wide (half an inch). After two or three weeks, they usually simply vanish, although in the interim they may have caused local itchiness. Occasionally, they may need to be surgically removed, if proving very troublesome to the individual dog.

DIARRHOEA

Cause and treatment much as gastritis (see below).

EAR INFECTIONS

Dogs have a long external ear canal, initially vertical then horizontal, leading to the eardrum, which protects the middle ear. If your Golden is shaking his head, then his ears will need to be inspected with an auroscope by a veterinary surgeon in order to identify the cause and to ensure the eardrum is intact. A sample may be taken from the canal, to be examined under the microscope and to be cultured (to identify causal agents). The vet will then prescribe appropriate ear drops containing antibiotic, anti-fungal agent and/or steroid.

Predisposing causes of otitis externa or infection in the external ear canal include: presence of a foreign body, such as a grass awn; ear mites, which are intensely irritating to the dog; previous infections, causing the canal's lining to thicken, narrowing the canal and reducing ventilation; and swimming – many Goldens simply adore swimming, but water trapped in the external ear canal can lead to infection, especially if the water is not clean!

Keep a close check on your Golden's ears to guard against possible infections.

Golden Retrievers cannot resist the water, but take care with an older dog who may become stiff in the joints after exercise.

FOREIGN BODIES

Internal: Items swallowed in haste without checking whether they will be digested can cause problems if they lodge in the stomach or obstruct the intestines, necessitating surgical removal. Acute vomiting is the main indication. Common objects I have seen removed include: stones from the garden, peach stones, babies' dummies, golf balls, and a lady's bra! It is possible to diagnose a dog with an intestinal obstruction across a waiting room, from a particularly 'tucked-up' stance and pained facial expression. These patients bounce back from surgery dramatically. A previously docile and compliant obstructed patient will return for a post-operative check-up, and literally bounce into the consulting room.

External: Grass awns are adept at finding their way into orifices such as a nostril, down an ear, and into the soft skin between two digits (toes). There, they start a one-way journey, due to the direction of their whiskers. In particular, I remember a grass awn that migrated from a hind paw, causing abscesses along the way, but not yielding itself up until it erupted through the skin in the groin.

GASTRITIS

This is usually just a simple stomach upset, most commonly in response to dietary indiscretion. In the case of a Golden, garbage gastritis is an even better description, because this breed is always on the look out for edible matter! Scavenging constitutes a change in the diet as much as an abrupt switch in the food given by the owner. Generally, a day without food, followed by a few days on a bland diet (such as cooked chicken or fish), or an appropriate prescription diet, fed little and often, should allow the stomach to settle. It is vital to wean the patient back on to routine food or else another bout of gastritis may occur.

HYPOTHYROIDISM (underactive thyroid gland)

This is one of the more common hormonal disorders in dogs, with the Golden seeming to be predisposed to it. Hypothyroidism manifests itself in the young adult as weight gain that does not respond to normal dietary manipulation. Other signs include lethargy and skin changes, such as dandruff and non-specific itchiness. Once diagnosed with blood tests, supplementing with thyroid hormone should reverse the changes.

JOINT PROBLEMS

It is not unusual for the older Golden Retriever to be stiff after exercise, particularly in cold weather and especially if coupled with a swim, which many Goldens simply love. See also 'inherited disorders'.

LUMPS

Regularly handling and stroking your dog will enable the early

Regular exercise and a well-balanced diet will keep your Golden fit and healthy.

detection of any lumps and bumps. These may be due to infection (abscess), bruising, multiplication of cells from within the body, or even an external parasite (tick). If you are worried about any lump you find, have it checked by a veterinary surgeon.

The Golden does seem to be predisposed to some specific neoplastic conditions, of which your veterinary surgeon will be aware. Mammary tumours are also common, and should be checked by a vet as soon as they are found.

MOULTING
The Golden's luxuriant coat needs a great deal of attention, which your Golden will enjoy if introduced to it on a regular basis from an early age. Grooming should be used as a time for pleasurable, close contact and reinforcement of the dog-owner relationship. However, the fact that we seek to maintain a constant, non-seasonal environment within our homes confuses the Golden into seemingly moulting all year round!

OBESITY
Being overweight predisposes the Golden to many other problems, such as diabetes mellitus, heart disease and joint problems. It is so easily prevented by simply acting as your Golden's conscience; ignore those eyes and feed according to your dog's waistline. The body condition is what matters qualitatively, alongside monitoring the individual dog's bodyweight as a quantitative measure. The Golden should, in my opinion, have at least a suggestion of a waist, and it should be possible to feel the ribs beneath only a slight layer of fat.

Neutering does not automatically mean that your Golden will be overweight. Having an ovario-hysterectomy does slow down the body's metabolic rate, and castration to a lesser extent. This therefore means that your dog needs less food. I recommend cutting back a little on the amount of food fed a few weeks before neutering to accustom your Golden to less food. If he looks a little underweight on the morning of the operation, it will help the veterinary surgeon as well as giving him a little leeway weight-wise afterwards. It is always harder to lose weight after neutering than before, because of this slowing in the body's inherent metabolic rate.

ROLLING
When a Golden rolls in fox muck, there is the potential for picking up a particular mite, resulting in sarcoptic mange. Fortunately, there are now specific licensed treatments.

TEETH
In the wild, dogs eat by gripping and killing prey with the canine teeth, biting off pieces of food with the incisors, and finally chewing with the molars. To be able to eat is vital for life, yet the actual health of the teeth is often overlooked; unhealthy teeth can create a predisposition to disease, and not just by reducing the ability to eat. The presence of infection within the mouth can lead to bacteria entering the bloodstream and then filtering out at major organs, with the potential for serious consequences. That is not to forget that simply having dental

pain can affect a dog's well-being, as anyone who has had toothache will confirm.

Many Goldens love simply carrying things such as logs, resulting in worn and broken teeth. Eating stones, a habit some dogs have, will also damage the teeth. Veterinary dentistry has made huge leaps in recent years, so that it no longer consists of extraction as the treatment of necessity. Good dental health lies in the hands of the owner, starting from the moment the dog comes into your care. Just as we have taken on responsibility for feeding, so we have also acquired the task of maintaining good dental and oral hygiene. In an ideal world, we should brush our dogs' teeth as regularly as our own. The Golden puppy who finds teeth-brushing to be a huge game and an excuse to roll around on the ground requires loads of patience, twice a day.

There are alternative strategies, ranging from dental chew-sticks to specially formulated foods, but the main thing is to be aware of your dog's mouth. At least train your puppy to permit having his teeth examined, which will not only ensure you are checking in his mouth regularly, but will also make your vet's job easier, when there is a real need for your dog to 'open wide!'

UVEAL CYST
You may notice one or more small, dark brown circular objects floating in the front of one or both of your Golden's eyes. In other breeds, they generally do

We are fortunate that the Golden Retriever is a sound breed with few inherited disorders.

not seem to cause any problems, but in the Golden they can occur with more serious eye conditions, so a vet's advice should be sought.

INHERITED DISORDERS
Any individual, dog or human, may have an inherited disorder by virtue of genes acquired from the parents. This is significant, not only for the health of that individual but also because of the potential for transmitting the disorder to their offspring and to subsequent generations, depending on the mode of inheritance. There are control schemes in place for some inherited disorders. For example, in the US, the Canine Eye Registration Foundation (CERF) was set up by dog breeders concerned about heritable eye disease. The foundation provides a database of dogs who have been examined by diplomats of the

American College of Veterinary Ophthalmologists. These are the major inherited disorders of concern in the Golden Retriever:

ELBOW DYSPLASIA
This is also called elbow osteochondrosis, and may first become apparent as a subtle forelimb lameness in the young juvenile Golden. The dog may also tend to sit with the affected leg slightly displaced, in order to bear less weight on the affected elbow. Flexion of the affected elbow during examination may be painful and resented! Older dogs with elbow dysplasia will be much stiffer than would be otherwise expected.

Elbow dysplasia is a progressive, degenerative, joint disease (arthritis) in response to one or more inherited features: ununited anconeal process, fragmented medial coronoid process, or osteochondritis of the medial humeral condyle. To be scored under the BVA/KC* and OFA*** schemes; each elbow is radiographed at a position of extreme flexion and assessed on a scale of zero (unaffected) to three (severely affected) once the dog has passed his first birthday. The highest score of the two elbows is given as the dog's scores, with breeders being advised to only breed from those with scores of zero or one. Each Golden can only have his elbows scored once in a lifetime.

Complementary therapies can have real benefits when used alongside orthodox treatment.

ECTROPION
(usually mild)
This is a rolling outwards of the eyelids, which usually resolves itself as the dog grows and matures. It may predispose to conjunctivitis, but it is usually cosmetic and rarely requires corrective surgery (CERF).

ENTROPION
This is an in-rolling of the eyelids. There are degrees of entropion, ranging from a slight in-rolling to the more serious case, requiring surgical correction, because of the pain and damage to the surface of the eyeball (CERF).

EPILEPSY
This condition is suspected to be inherited. It is often called juvenile epilepsy, because it manifests in the immature and young adult Golden (six months to three years old), with convulsions occurring singly or in clusters. It is very alarming as an owner to see your dog having a fit, because you feel utterly helpless. It is vital to note on a calendar when a fit or cluster of fits occurs, together with information about concurrent happenings (for example, family gathering, television switched on, fireworks, middle of the night). Even if a young adult Golden came to see me having had just one fit, I would be unlikely to start medication at once because 'every dog is allowed one or two fits'. If medication is given, it is impossible to assess whether or not the dog would have continued fitting. If it is needed to control the fits, then medication will, from the nature of the problem, be life-long.

HEREDITARY CATARACT
There is a dominant pattern of inheritance within this condition. A cataract is a cloudiness of the lens of the eye. In the Golden, this is the developmental form of hereditary cataract, occurring in the young or middle-aged dog. Due to the position of the lens changes in affected Goldens, fortunately blindness is rare. It is controlled under Schedule A of the BVA/KC/ISDS Scheme** in the UK, and CERF in the US. There is also a congenital form of hereditary cataract, where some form of lens opacity is present from birth. It is controlled under Schedule B of the BVA/KC/ISDS Scheme** in the UK, CERF in the US.

HIP DYSPLASIA
This is a malformation of the hip joints, causing pain, lameness and reduced exercise tolerance in the young Golden, and resulting in degenerative joint disease (arthritis) in the older dog. Each hip joint is scored on several features, to give a total of zero to 53 from a radiograph, taken with the hips and pelvis in a specified position. The radiographs are taken at the age of one year, under the BVA/KC Scheme*, and from two years of age in the US (OFA***).

MUSCULAR DYSTROPHY, CANINE
There is an X-linked inheritance of this condition in the Golden,

144

meaning that it tends to occur in male dogs, whilst bitches can carry the gene without undue effect. Its effects parallel those of Duchenne's muscular dystrophy in humans, such as weakness, muscular degeneration and difficulty swallowing.

OSTEOCHONDROSIS
Lameness becomes apparent from an early age, and affects the shoulder, elbow and hock joints (see also elbow dysplasia). This condition can be diagnosed from radiographs, and results in progressive degenerative joint disease or arthritis.

RETINAL DEFECTS
These defects include central progressive retinal atrophy (CPRA), generalised progressive retinal atrophy (GPRA) and multifocal retinal dysplasia (MRD), and are each controlled under Schedule A of the **BVA/KC/ISDS Scheme in the UK, CERF in the US.

TRICUSPID VALVE DEFECT (TVD)
There seems to be an increasing occurrence of TVD in the Golden. This is a congenital heart defect, where an affected dog is born with a malformed heart valve between the two chambers of the right side of the heart. The heart's ability to act as a pump depends on the integrity of its valves. A wide spectrum of effects is seen, ranging from a slight malformation (having little effect

With good care and management, your Golden Retriever will live a long, happy and healthy life.

on life-span), across to such a leaky valve that congestive heart failure develops while young. Blood leaking back through the valve causes turbulence in the blood flow, and the normally clear click as the valve closes is muffled. This is heard as a murmur when a stethoscope is placed on the chest wall, especially over the valve, so that a common time to first suspect TVD is when a vet examines the puppy as a first health-check, or prior to starting a vaccination course. A detailed ultrasound examination is needed to diagnose and stage the extent of the problem.

* British Veterinary Association/ Kennel Club Scheme
** British Veterinary Association/ Kennel Club/International Sheepdog Society Scheme
***Orthopedic Foundation for Animals, US

COMPLEMENTARY THERAPIES
There is a place for alternative therapies alongside and complementing orthodox treatment, under the supervision of a veterinary surgeon. However, because animals do not have a choice, there are measures in place to safeguard their welfare. All treatment must be under the direction of a veterinary surgeon, who has examined the patient and diagnosed the condition that needs treatment.

SUMMARY
As the owner of a Golden, you are responsible for his care and health. Not only must you make decisions on his behalf, you are also responsible for establishing a lifestyle for him that will ensure he leads a long and happy life. Diet plays an important part in this, as does exercise. For example, nutritional manipulation has a long history, but, for the domestic dog, it is only in recent years that the importance of so-called life-stage diets, which match the nutritional needs of the dog as he progresses through life, has been recognised.

Remember, as your Golden's owner, you are responsible for any decision made, so it must be as informed as possible. Always speak to your veterinary surgeon if you have any worries about your Golden. He is not just a dog; he will become a definite member of the family from the moment you bring him home.

THE CONTRIBUTORS

THE EDITOR: MAURICE SHORTMAN (BRIDGEFARM)

Maurice and his wife, Judy, obtained their first Golden Retriever in the early 1970s. Their initial litter, sired by Ch.Nortonwood Faunus out of Stromin Beryllium, produced Bridgefarm Harmoney, their first show bitch. Harmoney achieved many awards at Open and Championship Show level. She had an oustanding litter by Glennessa Escapade, which included Fin.& Est.Ch. Bridgefarm Glenleven. From Harmoney's second litter, to Starlance Huckleberry, came Bridgefarm Barleycorn and Bridgefarm Angelina. Barleycorn was awarded one CC and three RCCs together with 50 BOB at Open Shows. When mated to Ch. Moorquest Mugwump, she produced Sh. Ch. Rusway Sonnie Jim at Bridgefarm. Sonnie achieved 11 CCs, all with BOB, and seven RCCs, five BIS at Breed Championship Shows, and was the Top Winning Dog in the breed in 1991. All Bridgefarm's present dogs descend from Sonnie, including Rosaceae Indian Prince of Bridgefarm JW and one CC, Bridgefarm Home Alone, Shannonstyle Pollyanna of Bridgefarm JW and Bridgefarm Hopes And Dreams. The Bridgefarm stud dogs have sired Golden Retrievers that have achieved the status of Champion, Sh. Champion and JW winners in the UK, together with CAC and CACIB winners, Champions and Junior Champions in Europe and Asia. They have exported puppies to America, Belgium, Canada, Finland, France, Pakistan and Singapore. Maurice has judged Golden Retrievers at Championship Show level in Austria, Belgium, Denmark, Estonia, France, Germany, Holland, Italy, Switzerland and the UK, and also judged Gundog Groups and Best In Show at Open Show level in the UK and Overseas.

See Chapter Two: The First Golden Retrievers, Chapter Three: A Golden for your Lifestyle, and Chapter Seven: The Perfect Golden Retriever.

ANGELA COOPER (DIKEADAZE)

Angela has owned and showed Golden Retrievers since 1981. She has made up two Full Champions: Ch. Tokeida Outlaw's Hussy at Dikeadaze and Dikeadaze Wellington, and owned two Top Puppy in breed winners: Maurfield Mercury at Dikeadaze and Dikeadaze Not Guilty JW. All four also gained their Junior Warrants, as has Dikeadaze Sunkissed JW. Angela began working her dogs to the gun and in working tests in 1990, using the same dogs that she showed. She does between 70 to 90 days' picking up on shoots, and has won atall levels of working tests. She is now set to embark on field trialing her dogs.

See Chapter One: Getting to KnowGolden Retrievers.

GLENNIS HEWITSON (SERUILIA)

Glennis has been involved with dogs all her life – her mother bred Poodles, and from a very young age it was Glennis' job to look after the puppies. When Glennis married, a Golden Retriever bitch joined the family. 'Jodi' was a beautiful, very large, pale puppy; she stole their hearts, and from then onwards Glennis became deeply involved with the breed, from showing to breeding, and over the last 30 years, she has officiated as a judge, travelling all over the world. Glennis now lives in the West Country, very close to the sea, so her dogs have a wonderful life, walking on the beach and swimming in the sea.

See Chapter Four: The New Arrival.

DAWN ROSE (GAYTONWOOD)

Dawn had her first Golden Retriever when she was five years old. He was bred by her grandfather, and this dog started a lifelong love affair with the breed. Coming from a farming family, Dawn always went beating and picking up on local shoots and so when she started showing dogs, working them as well came naturally. Most of Dawn's Golden Retrievers work, and her ambition is to have a Golden capable of winning well in the show ring and the field.

See Chapter Five: The Best of Care.

JULIA BARNES

Julia has owned and trained Golden Retrievers for many years, and was a puppy socialiser for Dogs for the Disabled. A former journalist, she has written many books, including several on dog training and behaviour. Julia is indebted to Judy Shortman (Bridgefarm) for her specialist input.

See Chapter Six: Training and Socialisation.

ALISON LOGAN MA VetMB MRCVS

Alison qualified as a veterinary surgeon from Cambridge University in 1989. She has been in practice in her home town ever since, living with her husband, two children and Labrador Retriever, Pippin. Writing is increasingly taking up her time at home, contributing on a regular basis to *Veterinary Times, Veterinary Nurse Times, Dogs Today, Cat World* and *Pet Patter*, the PetPlan newsletter. In1995, Alison won the Univet Literary Award with an article on Cushing's disease, and she won it again (as the Vetoquinol Literary Award) in 2002, writing about common conditions in the Shar-Pei. In her spare time, she would like to play piano, take Pippin for day-long walks and work on the garden... but there are not enough hours in the day!

See Chapter Eight: Happy and Healthy.

USEFUL ADDRESSES

KENNEL & BREED CLUBS

UK
The Kennel Club
1-5 Clarges Street, London, W1J 8AB
Tel: 0870 606 6750
Fax: 0207 518 1058
Web: www.the-kennel-club.org.uk

To obtain up-to-date contact information for the following breed clubs, contact the Kennel Club:
- Berkshire Downs and Chilterns Golden Retriever Club
- Eastern Counties Golden Retriever Club
- Midland Golden Retriever Club
- Northern Golden Retriever Association
- Golden Retriever Club of Northumbria
- North West Golden Retriever Club
- Golden Retriever Club of Scotland
- Southern Golden Retriever Society
- South Western Golden Retriever Club
- Ulster Golden Retriever Club
- Golden Retriever Club of Wales
- Yorkshire Golden Retriever Club

USA
American Kennel Club (AKC)
5580 Centerview Drive,
Raleigh, NC 27606, USA.
Tel: 919 233 9767
Fax: 919 233 3627
Email: info@akc.org
Web: www.akc.org

United Kennel Club (UKC)
100 E Kilgore Rd, Kalamazoo,
MI 49002-5584, USA.
Tel: 269 343 9020
Fax: 269 343 7037
Web:www.ukcdogs.com/

The Golden Retriever Club of America, Inc.
Web: www.grca.org/

For contact details of regional clubs, please contact The Golden Retriever Club of America.

AUSTRALIA
Australian National Kennel Council (ANKC)
The Australian National Kennel Council is the administrative body for pure breed canine affairs in Australia. It does not, however, deal directly with dog exhibitors, breeders or judges. For information pertaining to breeders, clubs or shows, please contact the relevant State or Territory Controlling Body.

Dogs Australian Capital Teritory
PO Box 815, Dickson ACT 2602
Tel: (02) 6241 4404
Fax: (02) 6241 1129
Email: administrator@dogsact.org.au
Web: www.dogsact.org.au

Dogs New South Wales
PO Box 632, St Marys, NSW 1790
Tel: (02) 9834 3022 or 1300 728 022 (NSW Only)
Fax: (02) 9834 3872
Email: info@dogsnsw.org.au
Web: www.dogsnsw.org.au

Dogs Northern Territory
PO Box 37521, Winnellie NT 0821
Tel: (08) 8984 3570
Fax: (08) 8984 3409
Email: admin@dogsnt.com.au
Web: www.dogsnt.com.au

Dogs Queensland
PO Box 495, Fortitude Valley Qld 4006
Tel: (07) 3252 2661
Fax: (07) 3252 3864
Email: info@dogsqueensland.org.au
Web: www.dogsqueensland.org.au

Dogs South Australia
PO Box 844
Prospect East SA 5082
Tel: (08) 8349 4797
Fax: (08) 8262 5751
Email: info@dogssa.com.au
Web: www.dogssa.com.au

Tasmanian Canine Association Inc
The Rothman Building
PO Box 116
Glenorchy Tas 7010
Tel: (03) 6272 9443
Fax: (03) 6273 0844
Email: tca@iprimus.com.au
Web: www.tasdogs.com

Dogs Victoria
Locked Bag K9
Cranbourne VIC 3977
Tel: (03)9788 2500
Fax: (03) 9788 2599
Email: office@dogsvictoria.org.au
Web: www.dogsvictoria.org.au

Dogs Western Australia
PO Box 1404
Canning Vale WA 6970
Tel: (08) 9455 1188
Fax: (08) 9455 1190
Email: k9@dogswest.com
Web: www.dogswest.com

INTERNATIONAL
Fédération Cynologique Internationalé (FCI)/World Canine Organisation
Place Albert 1er, 13, B-6530 Thuin,
Belgium.
Tel: +32 71 59.12.38
Fax: +32 71 59.22.29
Web: www.fci.be/

TRAINING AND BEHAVIOUR

UK
Association of Pet Dog Trainers
PO Box 17, Kempsford, GL7 4WZ
Telephone: 01285 810811
Email: APDToffice@aol.com
Web: http://www.apdt.co.uk

Association of Pet Behaviour Counsellors
PO BOX 46, Worcester, WR8 9YS
Telephone: 01386 751151
Fax: 01386 750743
Email: info@apbc.org.uk
Web: http://www.apbc.org.uk/

USA
Association of Pet Dog Trainers
101 North Main Street, Suite 610
Greenville, SC 29601, USA.
Tel: 1 800 738 3647
Email: information@apdt.com
Web: www.apdt.com/

American College of Veterinary Behaviorists
College of Veterinary Medicine, 4474 Tamu, Texas A&M University
College Station, Texas 77843-4474
Web: http://dacvb.org/

American Veterinary Society of Animal Behavior
Web: www.avsabonline.org/

AUSTRALIA
APDT Australia Inc
PO Box 3122, Bankstown Square, NSW 2200,
Email: secretary@apdt.com.au
Web: www.apdt.com.au

Canine Behaviour
For details of regional behvaiourists, contact the relevant State or Territory Controlling Body.

ACTIVITIES

UK
Agility Club
http://www.agilityclub.co.uk/

British Flyball Association
PO Box 990, Doncaster, DN1 9FY
Telephone: 01628 829623
Email: secretary@flyball.org.uk
Web: http://www.flyball.org.uk/

USA
North American Dog Agility Council
P.O. Box 1206, Colbert,
OK 74733, USA.
Web: www.nadac.com/

North American Flyball Association, Inc.
1333 West Devon Avenue, #512
Chicago, IL 60660
Tel/Fax: 800 318 6312
Email: flyball@flyball.org
Web: www.flyball.org/

AUSTRALIA
Agility Dog Association of Australia
ADAA Secretary, PO Box 2212,
Gailes, QLD 4300, Australia.
Tel: 0423 138 914
Email: admin@adaa.com.au
Web: www.adaa.com.au/

NADAC Australia (North American Dog Agility Council - Australian Division)
12 Wellman Street, Box Hill South, Victoria 3128, Australia.
Email: shirlene@nadacaustralia.com
Web: www.nadacaustralia.com/

Australian Flyball Association
PO Box 4179, Pitt Town, NSW 2756
Tel: 0407 337 939
Email: info@flyball.org.au
Web: www.flyball.org.au/

INTERNATIONAL

World Canine Freestyle Organisation
P.O. Box 350122, Brooklyn, NY 11235-2525, USA
Tel: (718) 332-8336
Fax: (718) 646-2686
Email: wcfodogs@aol.com
Web: www.worldcaninefreestyle.org

HEALTH

UK
Alternative Veterinary Medicine Centre
Chinham House, Stanford in the Vale,
Oxfordshire, SN7 8NQ
Tel: 01367 710324
Fax: 01367 718243
Web: www.alternativevet.org/

British Small Animal Veterinary Association
Woodrow House, 1 Telford Way,
Waterwells Business Park, Quedgeley,
Gloucestershire, GL2 2AB
Tel: 01452 726700
Fax: 01452 726701
Email: customerservices@bsava.com
Web: http://www.bsava.com/

Royal College of Veterinary Surgeons
Belgravia House, 62-64 Horseferry Road, London,
SW1P 2AF
Tel: 0207 222 2001
Fax: 0207 222 2004
Email: admin@rcvs.org.uk
Web: www.rcvs.org.uk

USA
American Holistic Veterinary Medical Association
2218 Old Emmorton Road
Bel Air, MD 21015
Tel: 410 569 0795
Fax 410 569 2346
Email: office@ahvma.org
Web: www.ahvma.org/

American Veterinary Medical Association
1931 North Meacham Road, Suite 100,
Schaumburg, IL 60173-4360, USA.
Tel: 800 248 2862
Fax: 847 925 1329
Web: www.avma.org

American College of Veterinary Surgeons
19785 Crystal Rock Dr, Suite 305
Germantown, MD 20874, USA.
Tel: 301 916 0200
Toll Free: 877 217 2287
Fax: 301 916 2287
Email: acvs@acvs.org
Web: www.acvs.org/

AUSTRALIA
Australian Holistic Vets
Web: www.ahv.com.au/

Australian Small Animal Veterinary Association
40/6 Herbert Street, St Leonards, NSW 2065,
Australia.
Tel: 02 9431 5090
Fax: 02 9437 9068
Email: asava@ava.com.au
Web: www.asava.com.au

Australian Veterinary Association
Unit 40, 6 Herbert Street, St Leonards, NSW
2065, Australia.
Tel: 02 9431 5000
Fax: 02 9437 9068
Web: www.ava.com.au

Australian College Veterinary Scientists
Building 3, Garden City Office Park,
2404 Logan Road, Eight Mile Plains, Queensland
4113, Australia.
Tel: 07 3423 2016
Fax: 07 3423 2977
Email: admin@acvs.org.au
Web: http://acvsc.org.au

ASSISTANCE DOGS

UK
Canine Partners
Mill Lane, Heyshott, Midhurst, GU29 0ED
Tel: 08456 580480
Fax: 08456 580481
Web: www.caninepartners.co.uk

Dogs for the Disabled
The Frances Hay Centre, Blacklocks Hill,
Banbury, Oxon, OX17 2BS
Tel: 01295 252600
Web: www.dogsforthedisabled.org

Guide Dogs for the Blind Association
Burghfield Common, Reading, RG7 3YG
Tel: 01189 835555
Fax: 01189 835433
Web: www.guidedogs.org.uk/

Hearing Dogs for Deaf People
The Grange, Wycombe Road, Saunderton, Princes
Risborough, Bucks, HP27 9NS
Tel: 01844 348100
Fax: 01844 348101
Web: www.hearingdogs.org.uk

Pets as Therapy
14a High Street, Wendover, Aylesbury, Bucks.
HP22 6EA.
Tel: 01845 345445
Fax: 01845 550236
Web: http://www.petsastherapy.org/

Support Dogs
21 Jessops Riverside, Brightside Lane, Sheffield, S9
2RX
Tel: 01142 617800
Email: supportdogs@btconnect.com
Web: www.support-dogs.org.uk

USA
Therapy Dogs International
88 Bartley Road, Flanders, NJ 07836,.
Tel: 973 252 9800
Web: www.tdi-dog.o

Therapy Dogs Inc.
P.O. Box 20227, Cheyenne, WY 82003.
Tel: 307 432 0272.
Fax: 307-638-2079
Web: www.therapydogs.com

Delta Society - Pet Partners
875 124th Ave NE, Suite 101, Bellevue, WA
98005 USA.
Email: info@DeltaSociety.org
Web: www.deltasociety.org

Comfort Caring Canines
8135 Lare Street, Philadelphia, PA 19128.
Email: ccc@comfortcaringcanines.org
Web: www.comfortcaringcanines.org/

AUSTRALIA
AWARE Dogs Australia, Inc
PO Box 883, Kuranda, Queensland, 488..
Tel: 07 4093 8152
Web: www.awaredogs.org.au/

Delta Society -- Therapy Dogs
Web: www.deltasociety.com.au